IMAGES
of America

BAY RIDGE

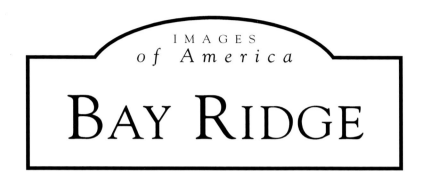

IMAGES
of America

BAY RIDGE

Bay Ridge Historical Society
Peter Scarpa, Lawrence Stelter,
and Peter Syrdahl

ARCADIA
PUBLISHING

Published by Arcadia Publishing
Charleston, South Carolina

Printed in the United States of America

Library of Congress Catalog Card Number: 2001089788

For all general information contact Arcadia Publishing at:
Telephone 843-853-2070
Fax 843-853-0044
E-mail sales@arcadiapublishing.com
For customer service and orders:
Toll-Free 1-888-313-2665

Visit us on the Internet at www.arcadiapublishing.com

CONTENTS

ACKNOWLEDGMENTS

The Bay Ridge Historical Society wishes to thank the following for their assistance in the preparation of this book: George Manos, Rita Unz, Norma Milde, Phillip and Loretta Stock, John Ryan, Peter Syrdahl, Louise Colavito, Jack and Elaine LaTorre, Eleanor Schiano, Tom Sarro, Joan Palisi and the estate of Dr. Joseph J. Palisi, Doris Cruz, Laura Rosen of MTA Bridges and Tunnels, Ken Cobb of the NYC Municipal Archives, Jim Modafferi, John Jankowski, Public School 102 Brooklyn, Dr. Jack Gabel, Charles Dono, and Sylvia Kramer.

INTRODUCTION

Farmhouses, summer cottages, and stately homes once dotted the shoreline of Bay Ridge; one could swim in the waters or fish in the bay or sail with high society from the yacht club. Small boats brought local farm produce from private piers to New York, or the produce was trekked over land to the Fulton Landing and then to the East River and Manhattan. First known as Yellow Hook, part of the township of New Utrecht, the area that became Bay Ridge was basically a rural community with homes clustered around St. Patrick's Church, near the landmark Fort Hamilton military post at its southern end and a small village at Ovington Avenue at its northern end. British troops once marched across these fields and bluffs, having landed at the Denyse pier near the current Verrazano Bridge. They marched up what is now Shore Road, turned right at Owl's Head Park, and went up 3rd Avenue to meet the American forces near Greenwood Cemetery in a battle now known to history as the Battle of Brooklyn.

While northern Brooklyn was rapidly becoming built up in the 19th century, Bay Ridge retained much of its rural character. This is reflected in the photographs taken by Samuel Winter Thomas, a keen observer of the area where he lived, at 3rd Avenue near 75th Street. Many Thomas photographs are in this collection, providing a unique image of Bay Ridge at the turn of the century. Born in Flushing in 1827, Samuel Winter Thomas and his brother William Thomas and their well-to-do families made Bay Ridge their home after the Civil War. In his leisure time, Samuel Winter Thomas enjoyed taking pictures of his Bay Ridge property and family, as well as of those of his neighbors and friends. It is our good fortune that he did. He died in 1913 in the home of his son Robert Thomas, on Ridge Boulevard and 75th Street. He is buried in Woodlawn Cemetery.

With the arrival of the subway in 1916, Bay Ridge increasingly began to change from its rural setting into a thriving community of row houses, stores, and trolley cars, as is reflected in some of the pictures in this book. In the process of constructing the Verrazano-Narrows Bridge and its access roadways, completed in 1964, a section of Bay Ridge around Fort Hamilton and to its north up to Dyker Heights was physically separated from the rest of the community. However, these areas remain in every other sense a part of Bay Ridge. Today, the Verrazano-Narrows Bridge has become a symbol of the community, perhaps most famously captured in the film *Saturday Night Fever*. In recent years "Restaurant Row" along 3rd Avenue has become a preferred destination for fine eating. The entire community is becoming more diverse, as new arrivals with Arabic, Asian, East European, and other ethnic heritages are mixing in with the many Irish, Italian, Greek, Scandinavian, and other populations already here. Bay Ridge, as its early residents also knew, is one of the best neighborhoods in New York City.

One

BECOMING BAY RIDGE: SCENES AND FACES OF THE PAST

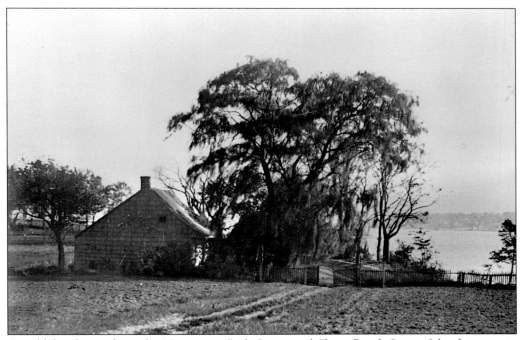

An old farmhouse faces the Narrows at 74th Street and Shore Road. Staten Island is seen in the distance. (Samuel Winter Thomas.)

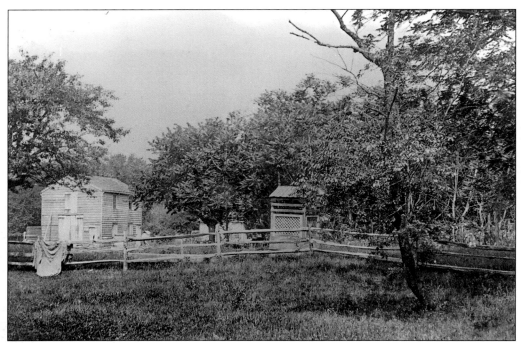

Farmhouse and out buildings stand beside a split rail fence at 3rd Avenue and 71st Street on June 10, 1893. (Samuel Winter Thomas.)

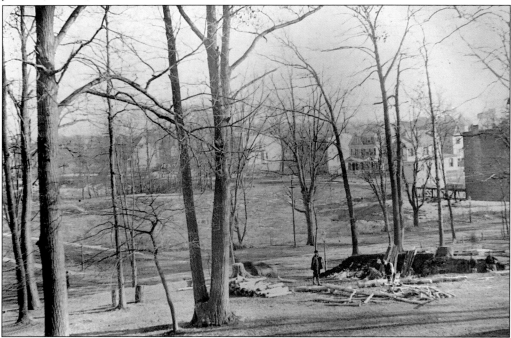

Looking east from his home, on 3rd Avenue, Samuel Winter Thomas surveyed the building of 76th Street on March 3, 1894. The houses in the distance faced 77th Street. The only store on 3rd Avenue displayed a piano advertisement.

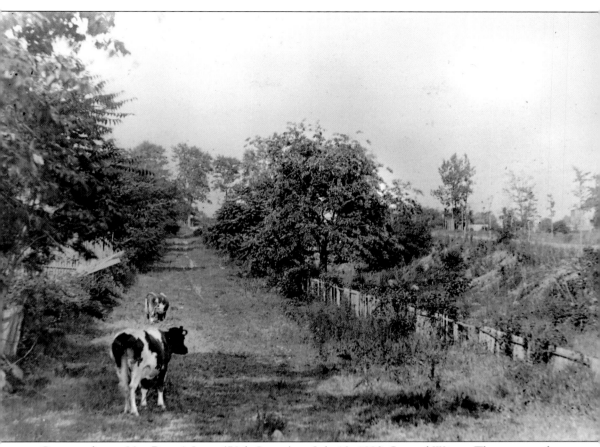

Cows trudge up Van Brunt's Lane (79th Street) on July 13, 1893. Samuel Winter Thomas stood at 2nd Avenue (Ridge Boulevard) and pointed his camera toward 3rd Avenue.

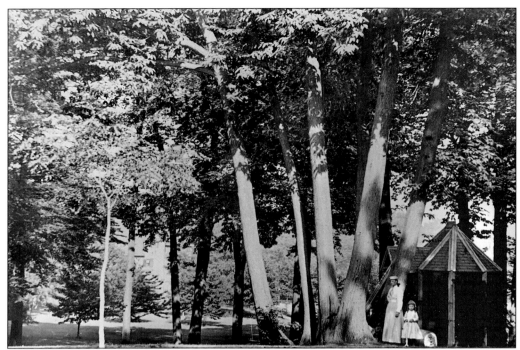

A woman and girl stand near chestnut trees at 76th Street and 3rd Avenue on August 15, 1893. (Samuel Winter Thomas.)

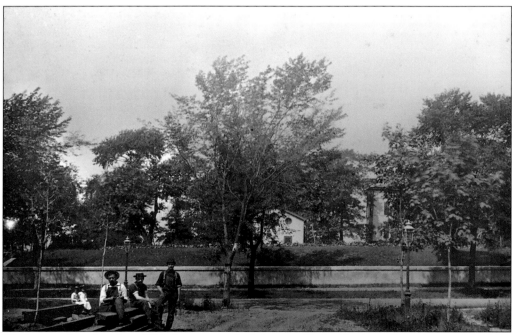

Workmen take a break on 77th Street near 2nd Avenue (Ridge Boulevard) on August 10, 1893. This photograph by Samuel Winter Thomas was taken looking west.

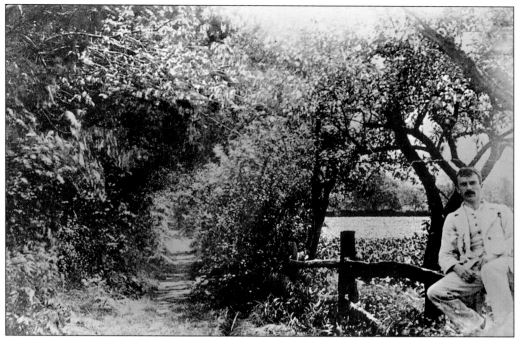

This man posed for the photographer at a country lane on the I.G. Bergen farm, which was on 73rd and 74th Street between 1st Avenue (Colonial Road) and what would become Narrows Avenue. (Samuel Winter Thomas.)

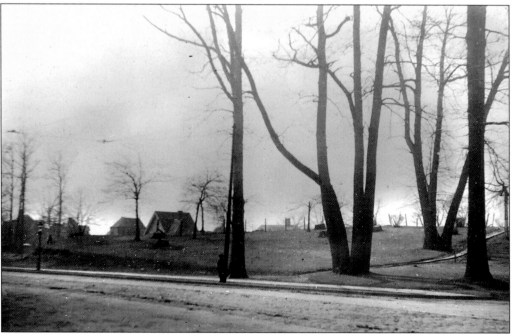

This scene shows 3rd Avenue and 76th Street on March 18, 1905. The Samuel Winter Thomas house is on the far right. (Samuel Winter Thomas.)

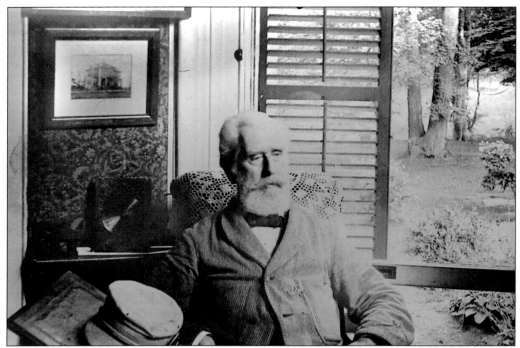

Samuel Winter Thomas (1827–1913) poses in his Bay Ridge home. The photograph of his home on the following page can be seen hanging on the wall to his right.

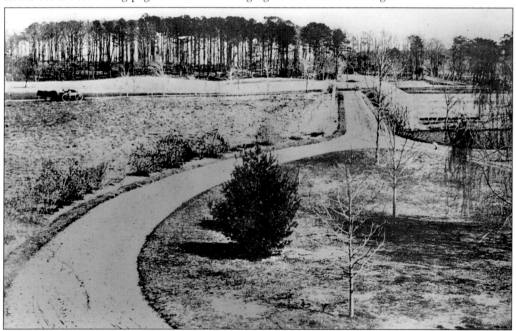

The William H. Thomas house, at 2nd Avenue and 77th Street, had this oval carriageway in 1865. The trees in the distance line 3rd Avenue between 75th and 77th Street, which was where Samuel Winter Thomas built his home a few years later. (Samuel Winter Thomas.)

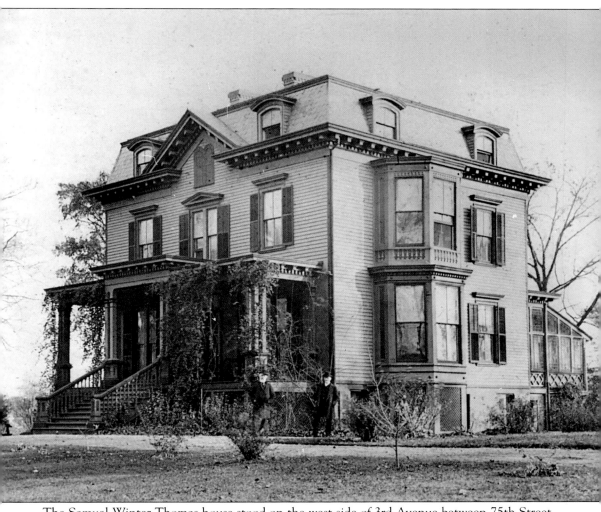

The Samuel Winter Thomas house stood on the west side of 3rd Avenue between 75th Street (now Bay Ridge Parkway) and 76th Street. This view was taken in 1890.

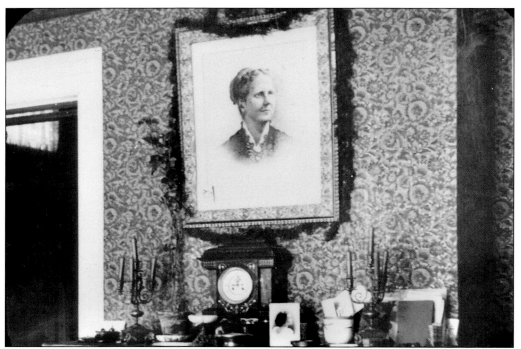

This is the mantel in the living room of the Samuel Winter Thomas house on January 11, 1894. (Samuel Winter Thomas.)

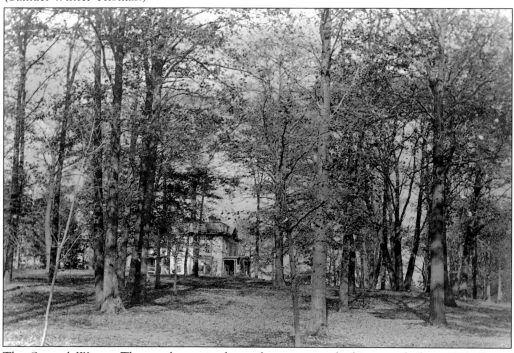

The Samuel Winter Thomas house is shown here as seen looking north from 77th Street through the trees that surrounded the estate in early 1900. (Samuel Winter Thomas.)

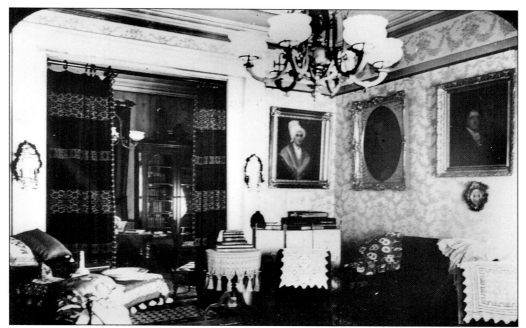

The parlor of the Samuel Winter Thomas house is captured here on January 28, 1894. Typical of Victorian décor, it included several large portraits of family members on its walls. (Samuel Winter Thomas.)

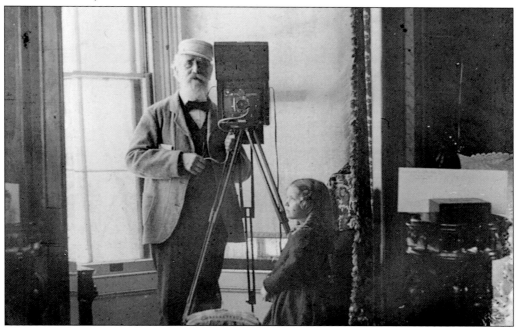

This view shows Samuel Winter Thomas at home with his camera and granddaughter. It was with this camera that Thomas was able to capture the many images of early Bay Ridge; part of his collection is included in this book. Left unpublished, it might otherwise have been lost to human memory. (Samuel Winter Thomas.)

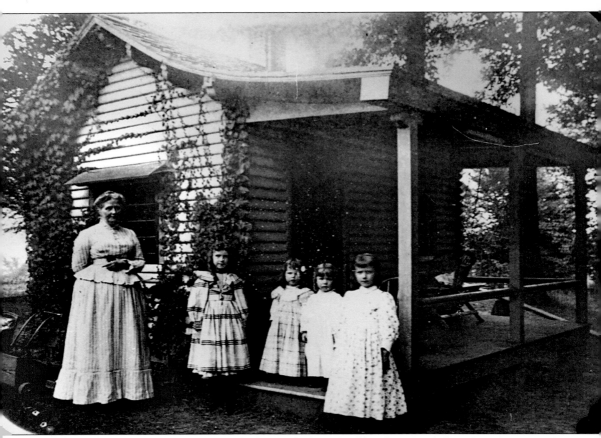

Samuel Winter Thomas built this playhouse for his granddaughters and their friends. It stood near 3rd Avenue and 76th Street. This picture was taken in 1891.

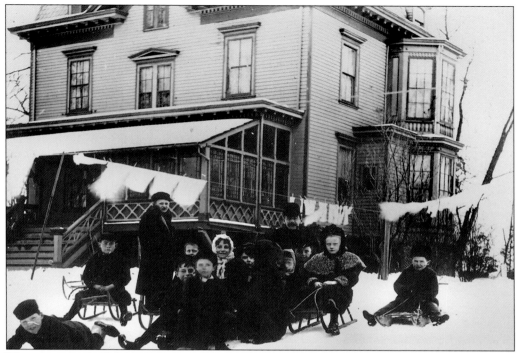

The servants had hung the laundry to dry at the Samuel Winter Thomas house on February 17, 1894. Meanwhile, these children and a few adults went coasting by sled. (Samuel Winter Thomas.)

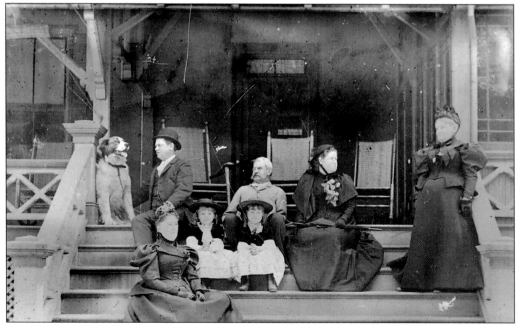

Members of this family group gaze in various directions from the back porch of the Samuel Winter Thomas home in 1894. (Samuel Winter Thomas.)

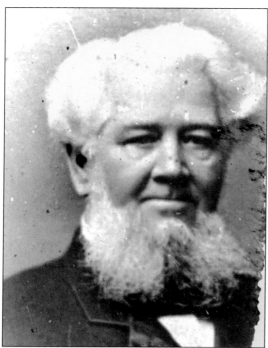

William H. Thomas (1817–1895), elder brother of Samuel Winter Thomas, founded the family cigar-importing business, with offices located at 25 Beaver Street and other lower Manhattan addresses. His large home stood between what became 75th and 76th Streets at the crest below 2nd Avenue (Ridge Boulevard.) (Samuel Winter Thomas.)

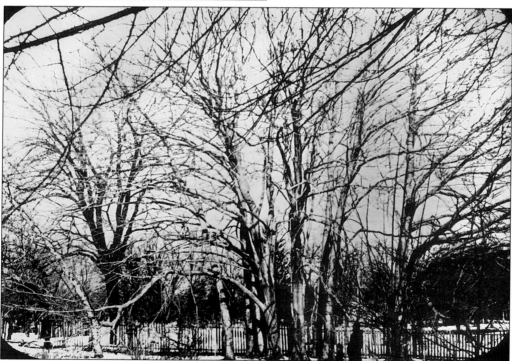

These beech trees on the Townsend Estate, at 75th Street and 2nd Avenue, were reported to be 200 years old. Early Bay Ridge residents referred to them as the "Twelve Apostles." Samuel Winter Thomas took this view of them on February 2, 1894.

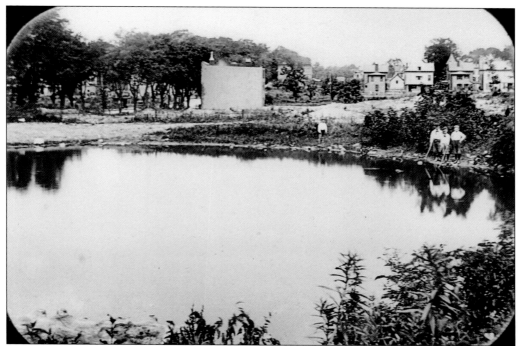

Several ponds dotted the landscape of early Bay Ridge. Here, the Van Brunt Pond can be seen in a view facing north toward 3rd Avenue between 81st and 82nd Streets on the Van Brunt estate. (Samuel Winter Thomas.)

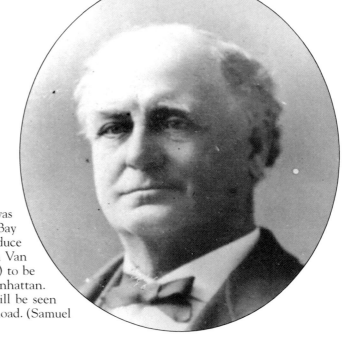

Jacques Holmes Van Brunt was a member of the prominent Bay Ridge family whose farm produce was regularly transported down Van Brunt's Lane (now 79th Street) to be shipped from their pier to Manhattan. A fragment of that pier can still be seen abutting the seawall on Shore Road. (Samuel Winter Thomas.)

21

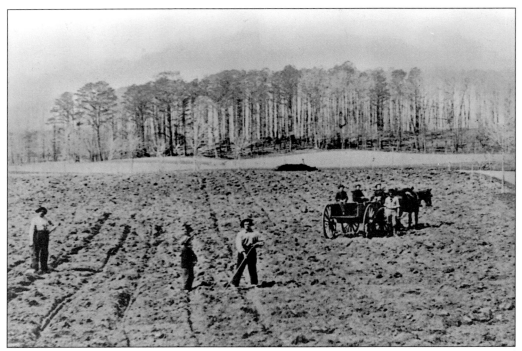

Farm workers pause in the planted fields near the William H. Thomas house at 77th Street and 2nd Avenue in 1865. (Samuel Winter Thomas.)

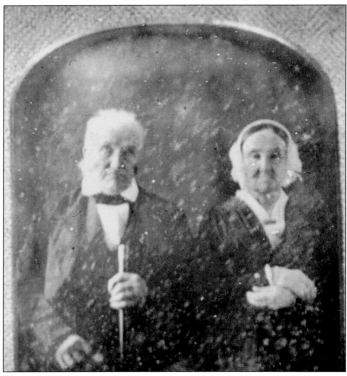

This daguerreotype is of the parents of J. Remsen Bennett, who lived at Shore Road and 77th Street. A Revolutionary War story about Mrs. Bennett relates that when the British were about to land to begin what became the Battle of Brooklyn ("Long Island"), she hurriedly grabbed the family laundry off the clothesline, quickly packed, and made off, with what she could carry, to safety in New Jersey. (Samuel Winter Thomas.)

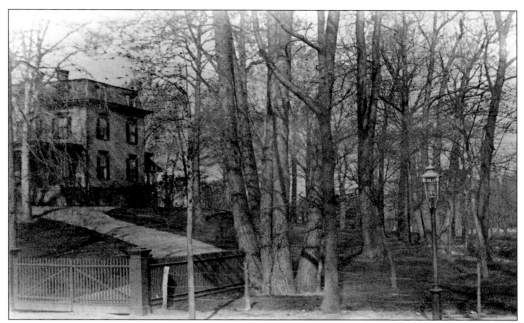

The Samuel Winter Thomas house stood slightly set back on the west side of 3rd Avenue between 75th and 76th Streets. The gas lamp near the entrance to his property was on 3rd Avenue, approximately where McAteer Florist is now located. (Samuel Winter Thomas.)

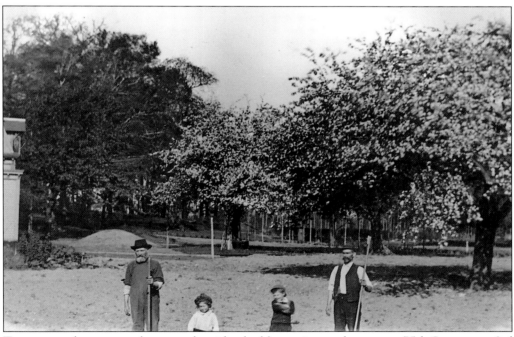

Two men and two young boys stand amidst the blossoming apple trees on 75th Street near 3rd Avenue. (Samuel Winter Thomas.)

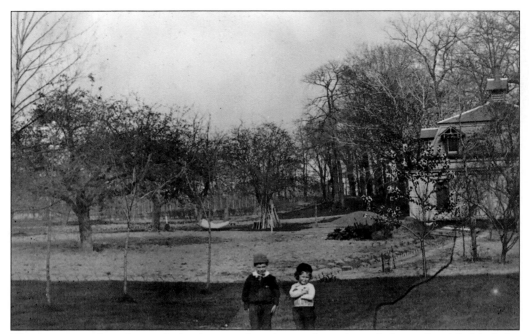

The same two boys have their picture taken in another view of the orchard behind the Samuel Winter Thomas house. Note the hammock strung between the trees. (Samuel Winter Thomas.)

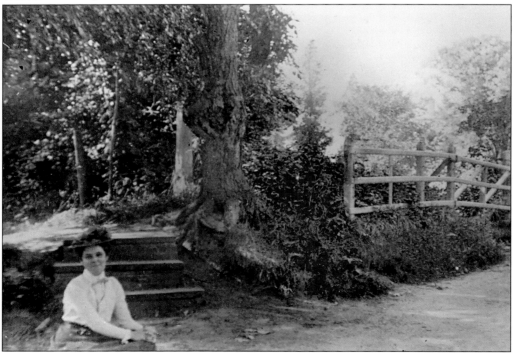

A smiling lady sits before a gnarled tree and steps at 2nd Avenue (Ridge Boulevard) and 70th Street before 1890. A Mrs. Andrews lent this photograph to Samuel Winter Thomas in 1905.

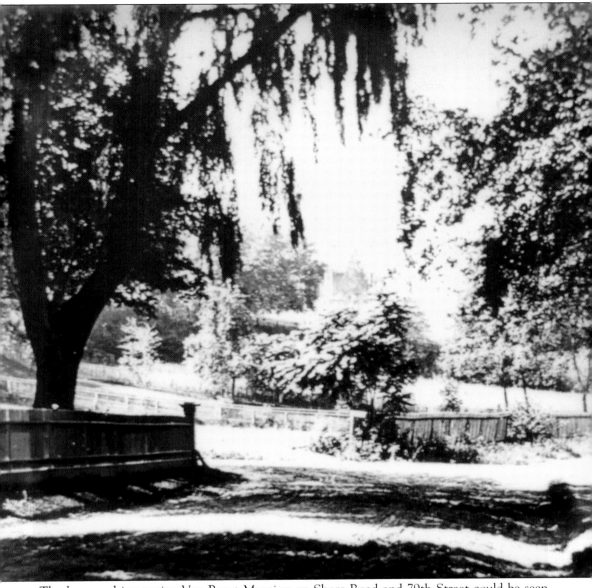

The large and impressive Van Brunt Mansion on Shore Road and 79th Street could be seen from many miles across the bay. (Samuel Winter Thomas.)

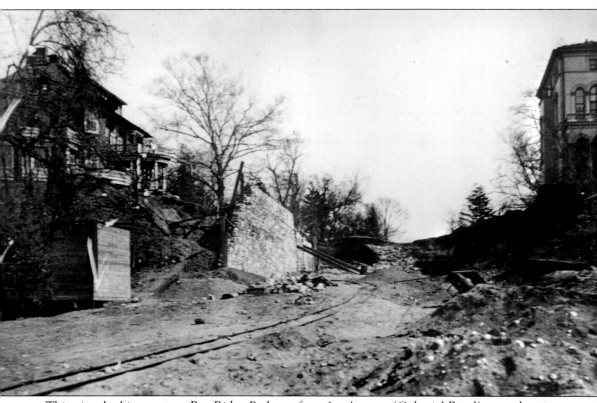

This view looking east on Bay Ridge Parkway from 1st Avenue (Colonial Road) was taken in 1904, shortly after the road had been carved out to become 75th Street. "The Ridge," as the home of Chris Shultheis on the left was later known, was demolished in 1981 and replaced by 14 three-family row houses. (Samuel Winter Thomas.)

Two

BUILDING BAY RIDGE: HOMES AND ESTATES BY THE BAY

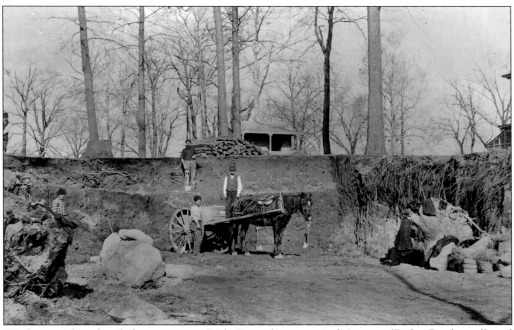

Workmen take a break from opening 76th Street between 2nd Avenue (Ridge Boulevard) and 3rd Avenue to have their picture taken by Samuel Winter Thomas on March 7, 1894. The Samuel Winter Thomas house is to the right and the playhouse is in the middle.

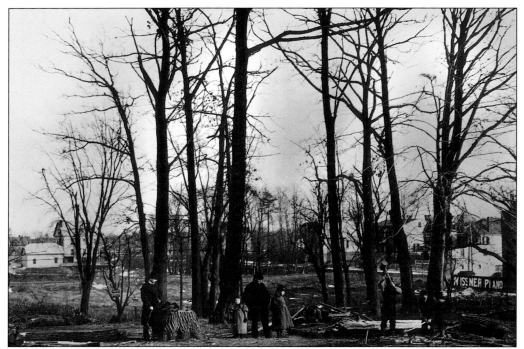

The photographer's family observes the opening of 76th Street on February 24, 1894. In this view looking east, the houses in the distance face 77th Street. The building with the Wissner Piano sign is on 3rd Avenue. (Samuel Winter Thomas.)

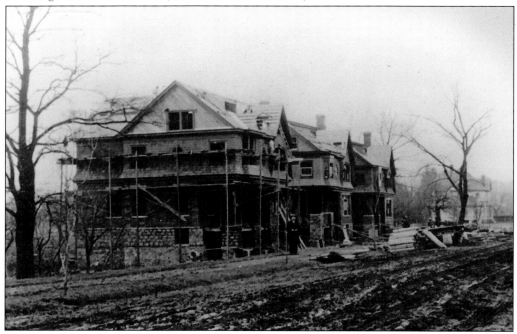

This view was taken looking west at the south side of 74th Street from near 3rd Avenue on January 5, 1894. (Samuel Winter Thomas.)

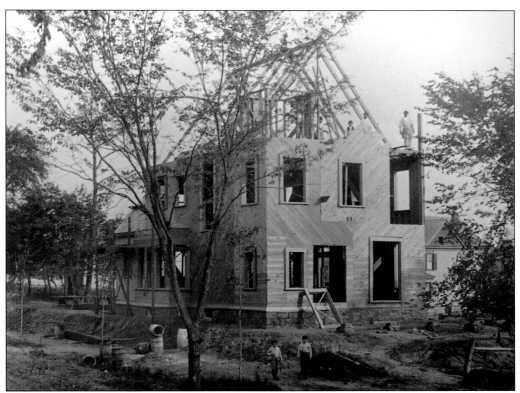

Workmen at this house under construction at 77th Street and 2nd Avenue (Ridge Boulevard) pose for Samuel Winter Thomas, and posterity, on September 11, 1893.

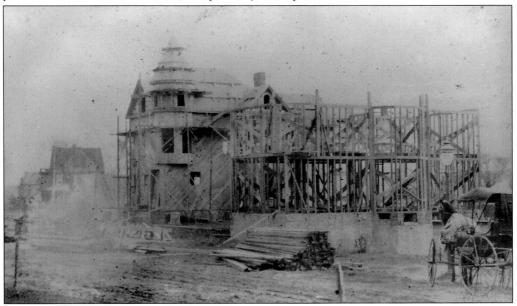

A buggy with its blanketed horse waits before these houses under construction on 76th Street west of 4th Avenue on November 7, 1893. (Samuel Winter Thomas.)

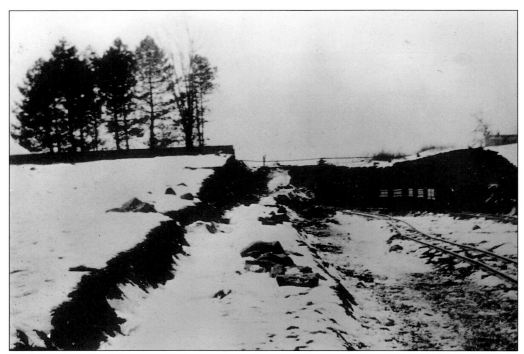

The grading of 2nd Avenue (Ridge Boulevard) is seen here near 82nd Street. (Samuel Winter Thomas collection from F.N. Doubleday negative.)

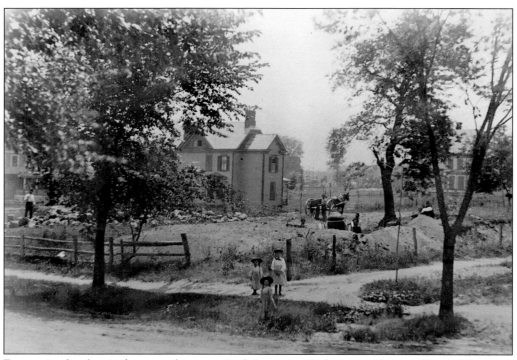

Excavation has begun for a new home on 2nd Avenue at 77th Street.(Samuel Winter Thomas.)

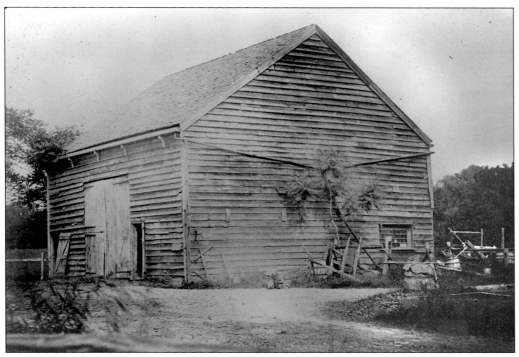

It is perhaps difficult to imagine, but barns like this were once typical in Bay Ridge. (Samuel Winter Thomas.)

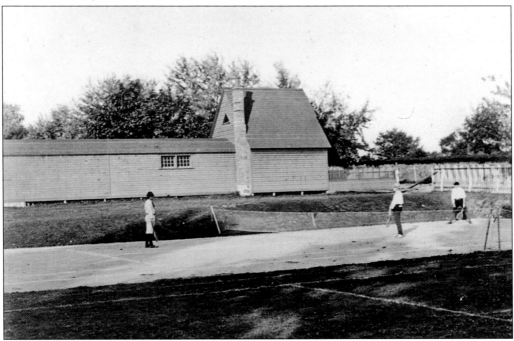

There was a tennis court and bowling alley at the Parkinson house at 2nd Avenue and 68th Street. (Samuel Winter Thomas.)

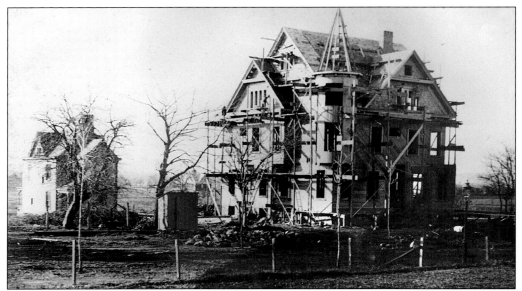

On January 19, 1894, this house was under construction on the south side of 77th Street between 2nd Avenue (now Ridge Boulevard) and 3rd Avenue. (Samuel Winter Thomas.)

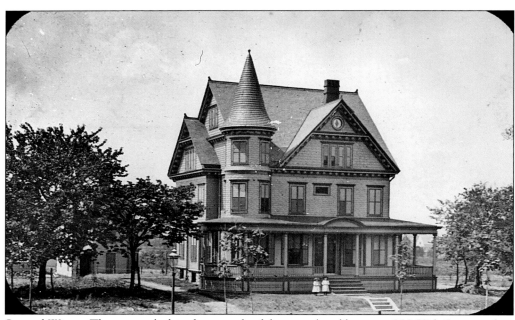

Samuel Winter Thomas took this photograph of the completed house at 220 77th Street in late 1894. He often included his grandchildren in his photographs.

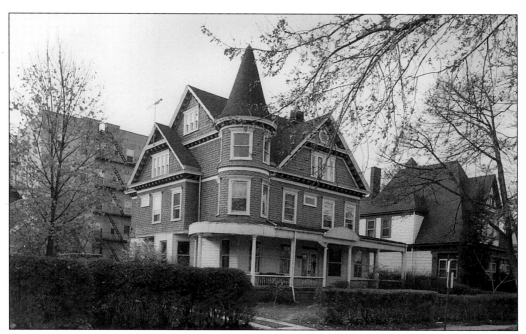

A recent view shows 220 77th Street, which still looks much as it did when it was built 107 years ago. (Perlmutter, Bay Ridge Historical Society.)

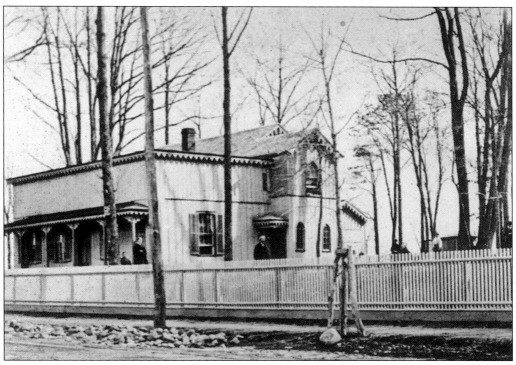

This roadhouse once stood on 3rd Avenue between 76th and 77th Streets. (Samuel Winter Thomas.)

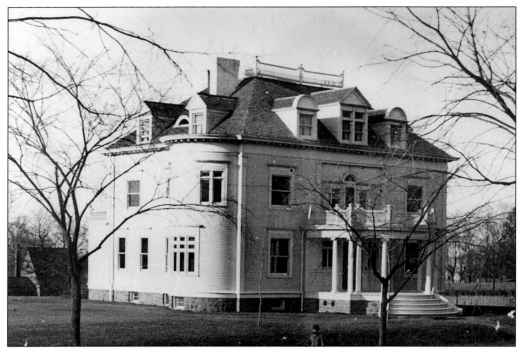

The Parkinson house on 2nd Avenue and Church Lane (68th Street) is seen here in 1894. (Samuel Winter Thomas.)

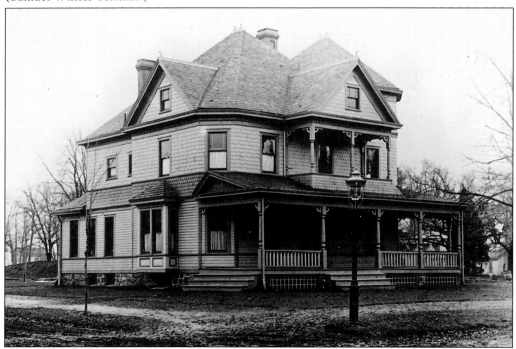

This was the Dr. Bellum house on 2nd Avenue (Ridge Boulevard) and 74th Street. (Samuel Winter Thomas.)

This gatehouse stood outside the B.L. Townsend estate at 3rd Avenue and 74th Street in 1865. (Samuel Winter Thomas.)

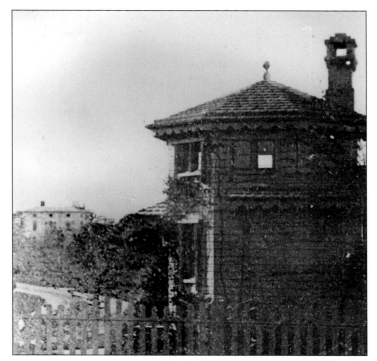

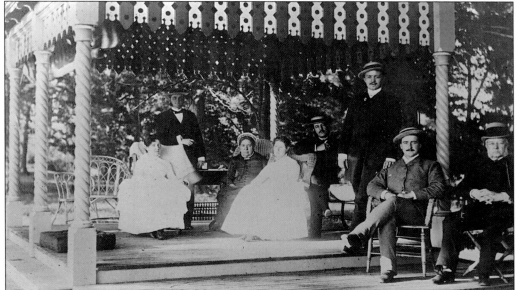

Family members are seen relaxing in the shade of this typically ornate gazebo at the Townsend family mansion, which stood at 2nd Avenue (Ridge Boulevard) near 74th Street. On Dec. 16, 1853, Benjamin C. Townsend was one of many prominent residents of the area, then known as Yellow Hook, who voted to change the name of their community to Bay Ridge rather than suffer the undesirable and certainly unfashionable association the word "yellow" had taken on as a result of recent outbreaks and the continuing threat of yellow-fever epidemics. Happily, the name has been Bay Ridge ever since. (Samuel Winter Thomas.)

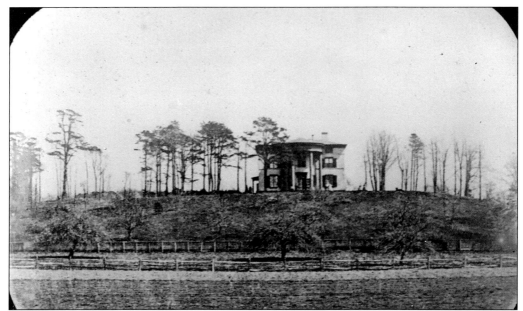

This house stood on the hill above 1st Avenue (Colonial Road) and 76th Street in 1865. The location is one of only two in Bay Ridge that were not graded through (the other being 74th Street) and has large staircases connecting the upper and lower portions of the street. This hill marks the terminal moraine for the East Coast and the southernmost deposit of land pushed ahead of the glacial ice caps that had covered much of North America during the Ice Age, before that ice finally began to melt and recede. (Samuel Winter Thomas.)

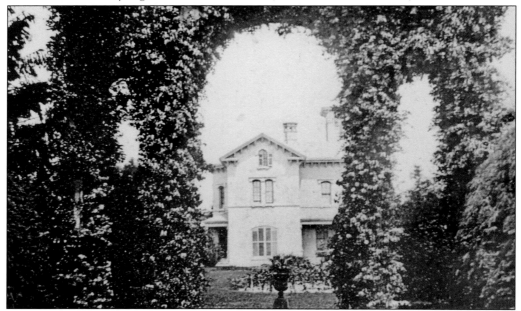

This view was taken looking from 84th to 85th Streets between 2nd and 3rd Avenues. It shows the arch at the Bullocke house, which was famous for its clinging wisteria and other vines. (Samuel Winter Thomas.)

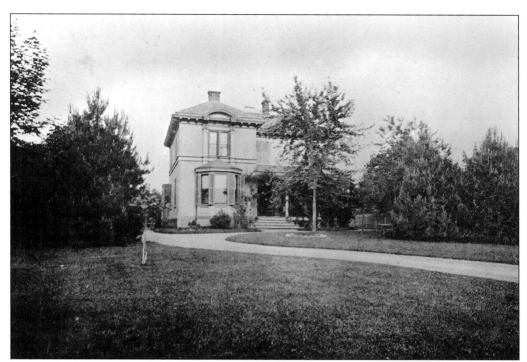

One of Samuel Winter Thomas's well-to-do neighbors was the Bullocke family. The Bullocke home stood west of 3rd Avenue near 84th Street. (Samuel Winter Thomas.)

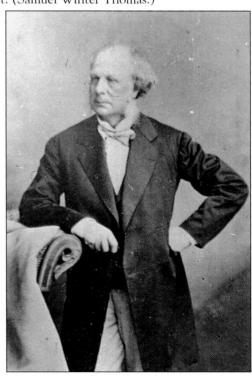

John Bullocke is seen here in 1905.

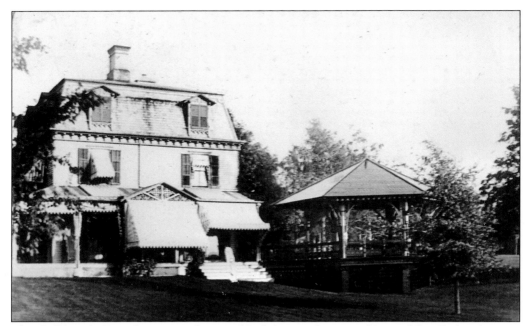

The William A. Perry house stood west of 2nd Avenue between 71st and Bay Ridge Avenue. Perry Terrace is named after the family. The photograph was taken in 1883. (Samuel Winter Thomas.)

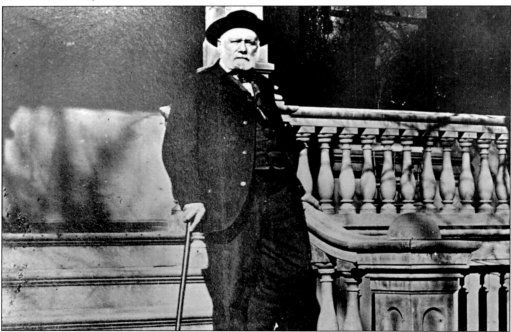

Included in the Samuel Winter Thomas collection is this picture of George S. Gelston who died in 1891. His home stood overlooking the bay at the intersection of Shore Road and 3rd Avenue. Gelston Avenue, which runs from 86th Street to 94th Street, was named for his family.

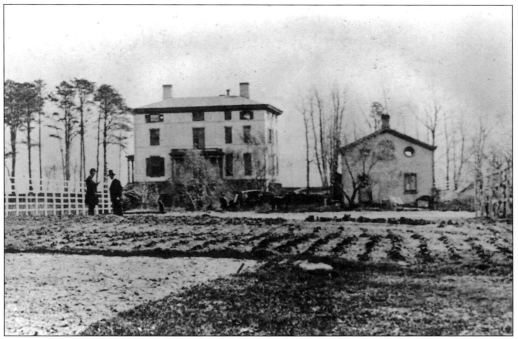

The William H. Thomas house, at 77th Street and 2nd Avenue, is seen in this 1865 photograph. (Samuel Winter Thomas.)

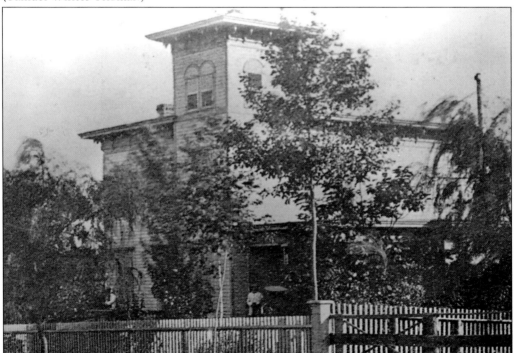

The Otto Heinigke house stood on Ovington Avenue east of 4th Avenue in 1859. Heinigke was a noted stained glass designer and manufacturer. (Samuel Winter Thomas.)

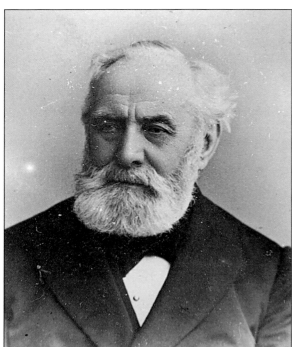

Joseph Wild posed for this photograph in 1905. Wild lived near the present 69th Street pier, with property extending toward the present Owl's Head Park.

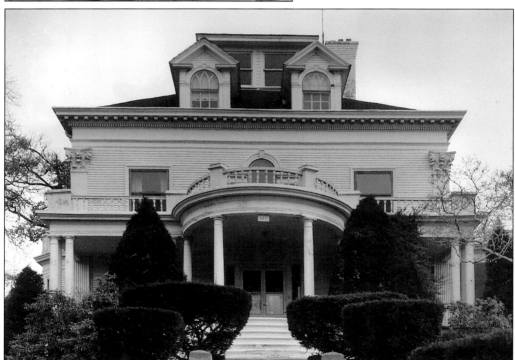

This house at 8311 Ridge Boulevard, one of the grand mansions of old, still occupies the knoll on the east side of Ridge Boulevard near 84th Street. (Perlmutter, Bay Ridge Historical Society.)

This photograph of Mary Devine was taken in 1910.

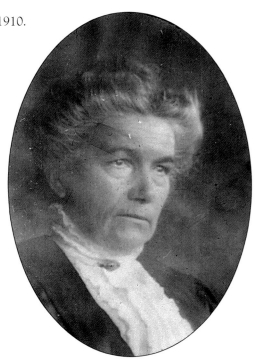

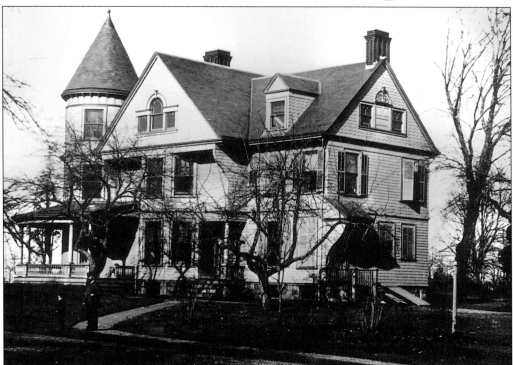

The south side of the P. Schenck Bogart residence is seen here as it looked in January 1894. (Samuel Winter Thomas.)

Rev. J.A. Aspinwall posed for this photograph on June 15, 1905. The photograph was to be used by the Ridge Club in an announcement for an illustrated lecture entitled "Beautiful Old Bay Ridge."

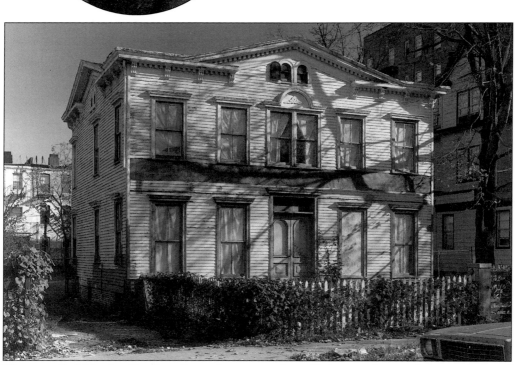

The so-called Harriet Beecher Stowe house stood on Ovington Avenue between 3rd and 4th Avenues. The famous author never lived here nor in Brooklyn, yet Ovington family members were noted abolitionists. The house was razed in 1984. (Perlmutter, Bay Ridge Historical Society.)

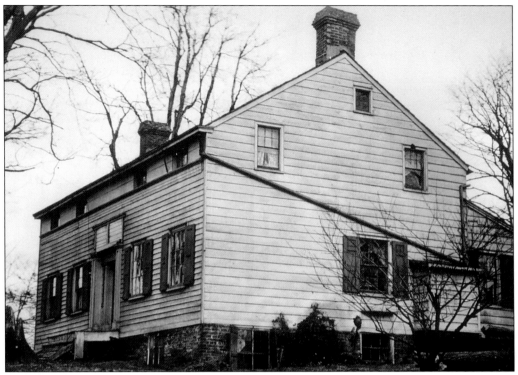

The Denyse house faced the shore near Fort Hamilton. (Tom Sarro Archives.)

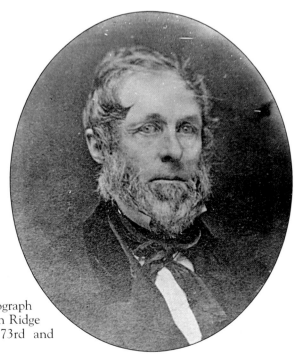

George Fletcher posed for this photograph in 1905. His home was located between Ridge Boulevard and Colonial Road and 73rd and 74th Streets.

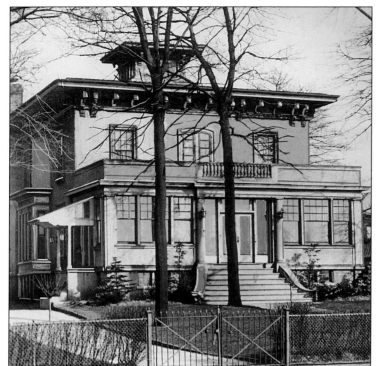

This Italianate-style house at Shore Road and 91st Street was one of several Van Brunt mansions along the Shore Road. (Bay Ridge Historical Society.)

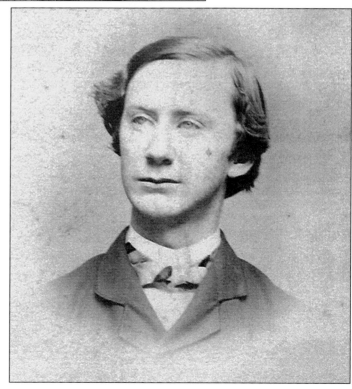

1st Lt. Bergen Van Brunt was a Civil War veteran of the New York State 131st Regiment. He enlisted in September 1862, at the age of 23, and served until he was discharged for disability in March 1865. (Tom Sarro Archives.)

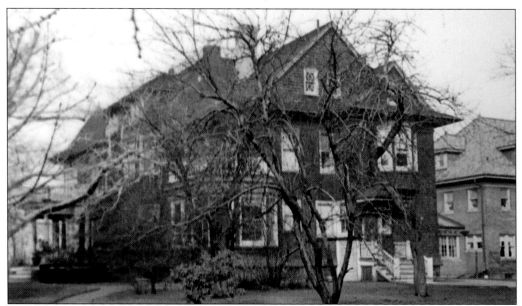

"The Ridge" mansion, or the Shultheis house, stood at 125 Bay Ridge Parkway (75th Street) in 1941. (Courtesy of NYC Municipal Archives.)

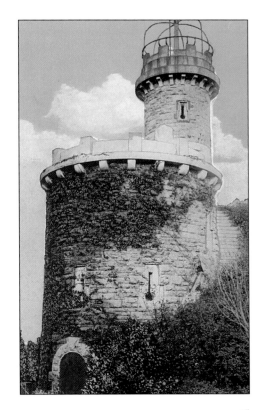

The Bliss Tower overlooked the bay from what was once the Honorable Senator Murphy's grand estate, later the Bliss estate. It survived into the middle of the 20th century in what some old-timers may still refer to as Bliss Park, officially Owl's Head Park. (Peter Syrdahl.)

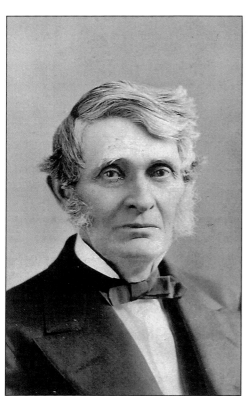

Henry Cruise Murphy, one-time mayor of the city of Brooklyn, former New York state senator, and U.S. minister to Holland, resided for many years at his Bay Ridge estate, where Owl's Head Park is today. The estate was named after the owls that were seen on the grounds and, in particular, after the owl images that Murphy had constructed on the gateposts to his property. (Tom Sarro Archives.)

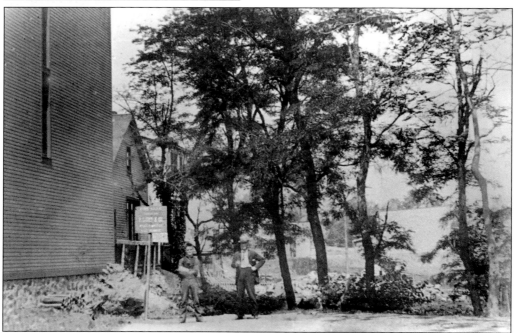

This property at 3rd Avenue west of 67th Street was for sale. Samuel Winter Thomas noted it was "the site of the entrance to Senator Murphy's place."

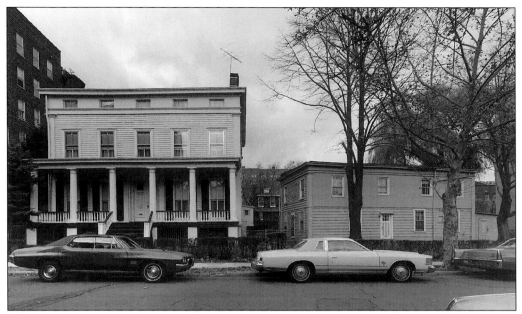

This view shows the Farrell House (left) and the Bennett barn (right), on 95th Street between Shore Road and Marine Avenue. The house, built *c.* 1845, was declared a NYC landmark in 1999. The construction history of the barn could not be firmly dated and, thus, that building was demolished in 2000. (Perlmutter, Bay Ridge Historical Society.)

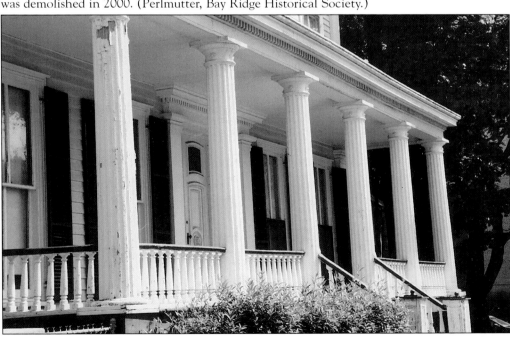

The front of the Farrell House faces south today. The house was turned from its original west orientation overlooking the bay after Mrs. Farrell could no longer bear the grief of viewing the ships and water that had recently claimed the lives of both her husband and son at sea. (Peter Syrdahl.)

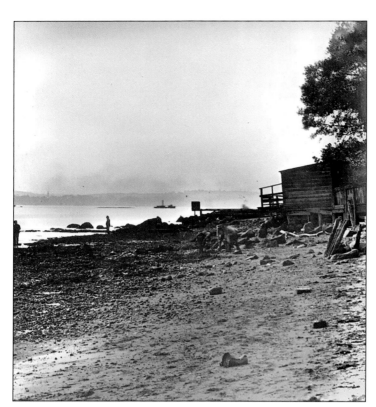

The Wren family cottage stood at 70th Street and the Bay Ridge beach. (Samuel Winter Thomas.)

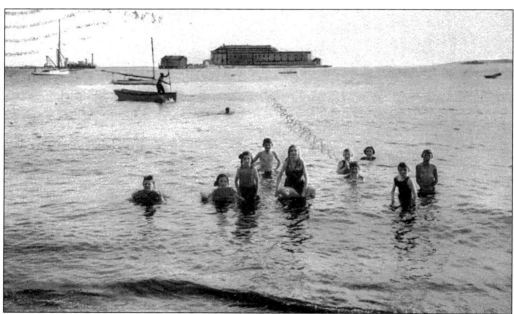

This postcard shows children swimming in the Narrows c. 1909. Fort Lafayette is in the background; its site is now the base of the Brooklyn tower of the Verrazano Bridge. (Phillip and Loretta Stock.)

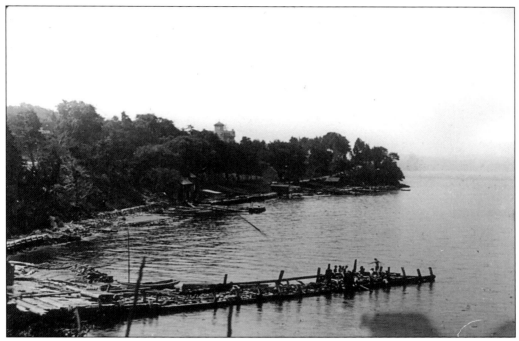

This photograph of the Tunis G. Bergen dock was taken looking south from 73rd to 79th Street in 1860. (Samuel Winter Thomas.)

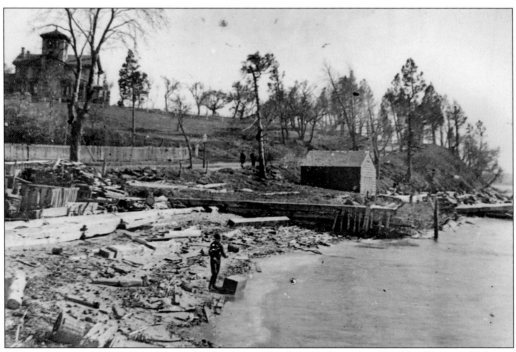

This view of Shore Road and 77th Street looks south toward 79th Street. (Samuel Winter Thomas.)

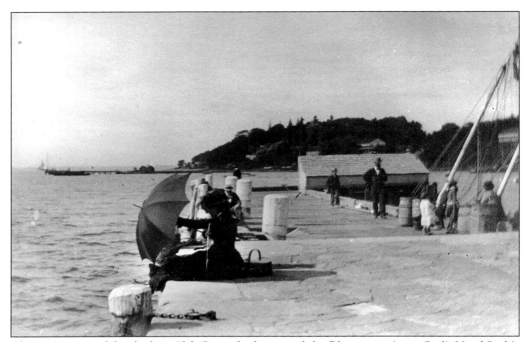

This 1883 view of the dock at 65th Street looks toward the Bliss estate (now Owl's Head Park). The Owl's Head Water Pollution Control Plant, which now sits near the base of that hill, was put into service in 1952. (Samuel Winter Thomas.)

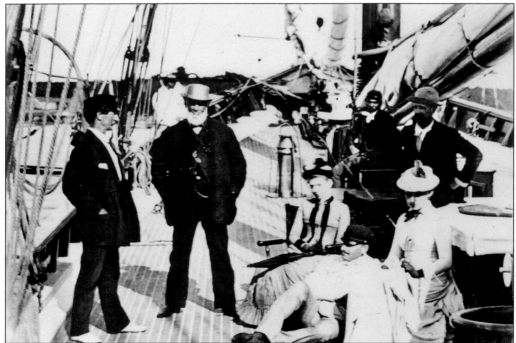

This scene shows a group of men and women aboard the yacht *Rambler* at the 69th Street anchorage. (Samuel Winter Thomas.)

George T. Hope was a distinguished Bay Ridge resident. He posed for this photograph, taken by Samuel Winter Thomas, in 1905.

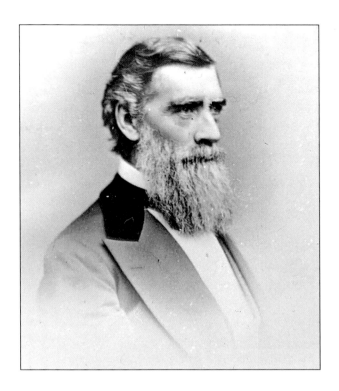

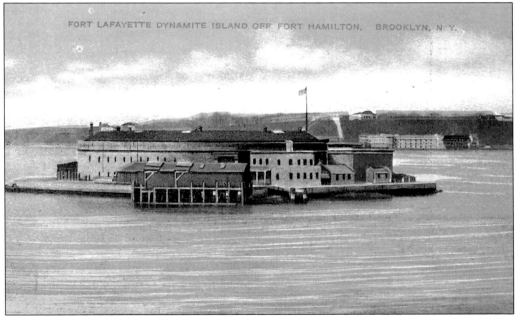

This postcard shows Fort Lafayette, also known as Dynamite Island, c. 1909. During the Civil War, this fort was used as a prison. Among its Confederate Army prisoners was William Fitzhugh (Rooney) Lee, the son of nearby Fort Hamilton's one-time commandant, Gen. Robert E. Lee. (Phillip and Loretta Stock.)

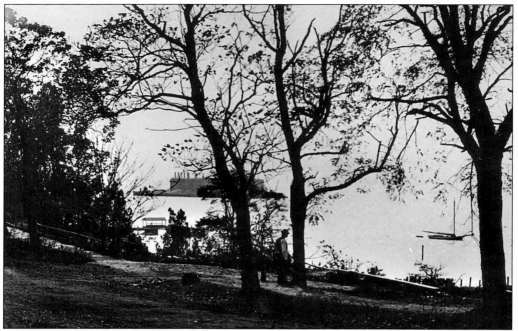

This view of Fort Lafayette from 92nd Street and Shore Road was captured by Samuel Winter Thomas in the 1890s. The Brooklyn tower of the Verrazano Bridge now stands on the site of the fort. (Samuel Winter Thomas.)

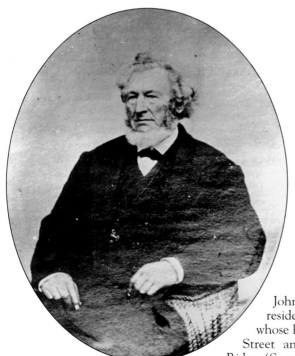

John Bennett was an old-time Bay Ridge resident. He was one of the many Bennetts whose homes were located on what is now 79th Street and in other locations throughout Bay Ridge. (Samuel Winter Thomas.)

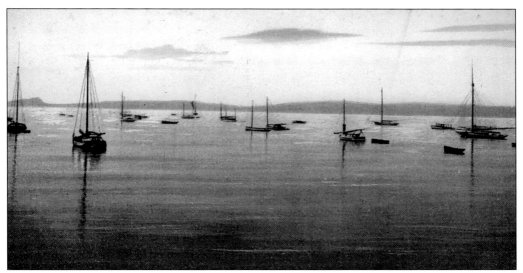

This postcard reflects a tranquil view of the bay at Bay Ridge. (Phillip and Loretta Stock.)

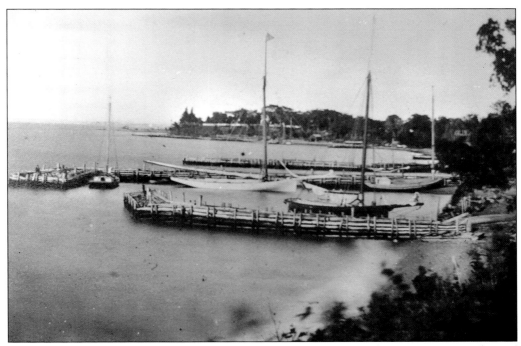

This view was taken looking north from 79th Street and Shore Road in 1879. Farmers shipped produce that was grown in Bay Ridge and nearby communities to markets in New York City. (Samuel Winter Thomas.)

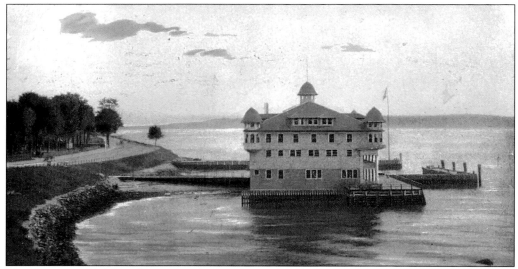

The Crescent Club Boathouse stood at 83rd Street and Shore Road (Ed Milanese.)

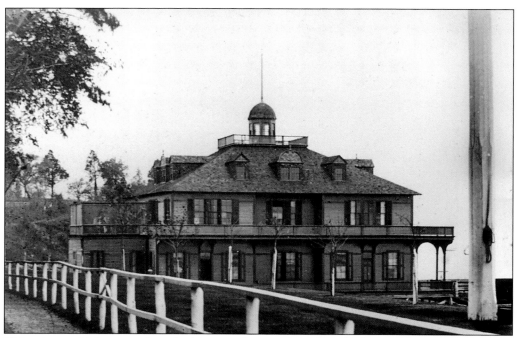

This view, which was taken looking south on Shore Road, shows the second Crescent Boathouse. (Samuel Winter Thomas.)

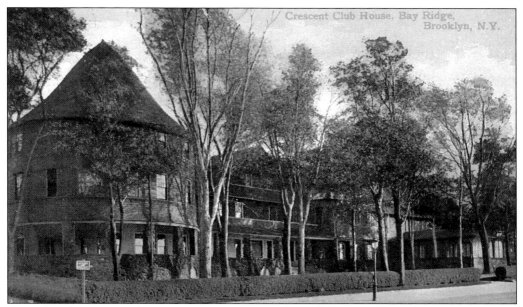

Pres. Theodore Roosevelt was an interested spectator at the first Davis Cup tennis match held at the Crescent Clubhouse, now the site of Fort Hamilton High School. (Peter Syrdahl.)

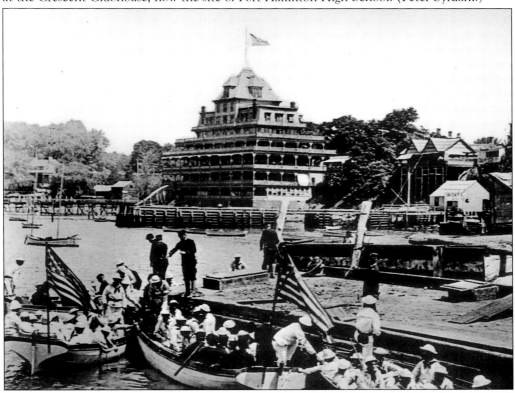

Sailors on liberty are shown near Fort Hamilton. The tall structure is the Grand View Hotel. (Samuel Winter Thomas.)

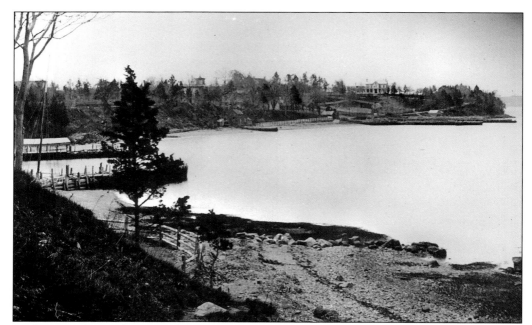

Looking south on Shore Road from 73rd Street, Samuel Winter Thomas captured this view c. 1877. (Samuel Winter Thomas.)

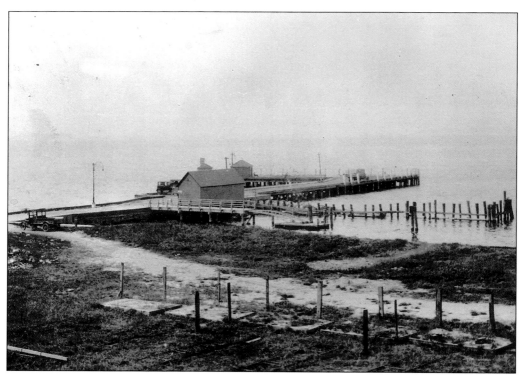

It was at Denyse Wharf in 1776 that the British landed to commence the Battle of Brooklyn, "Long Island." Here, the wharf is seen in an October 1, 1925 photograph.

Jacob J. Moore poses for an early portrait. (Samuel Winter Thomas.)

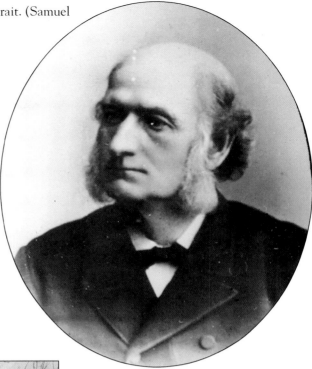

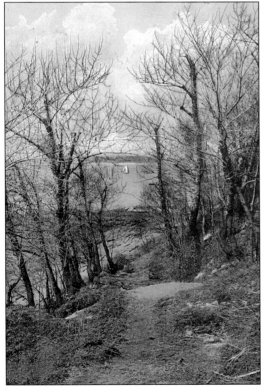

The scene shows the shore near Fort Hamilton c. 1910. (Peter Syrdahl.)

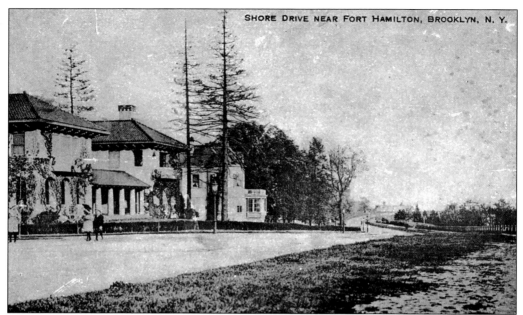

This postcard shows the Shore Road home of flamboyant New Yorker "Diamond Jim" Brady and the actress Lillian Russell in 1912. Fontbonne Hall Academy is now at this site. (Peter Syrdahl.)

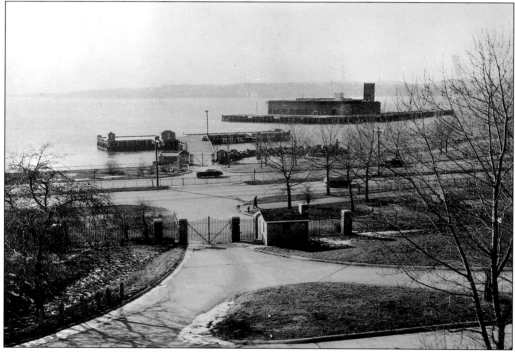

This view of Denyse Wharf and Fort Lafayette was taken from Fort Hamilton on January 18, 1955. During the Colonial era, the ferry service from this wharf served as a major north–south link in the nation's transportation network. (Bay Ridge Historical Society.)

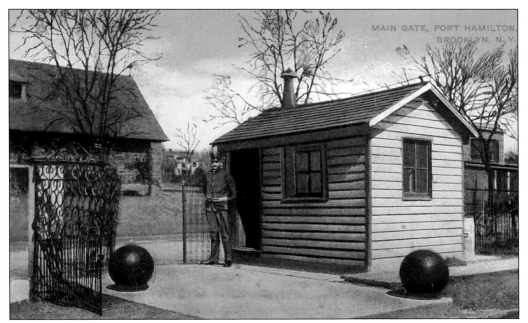

This photo postcard shows the gatehouse at Fort Hamilton, *c.* 1910 (Phillip and Loretta Stock.)

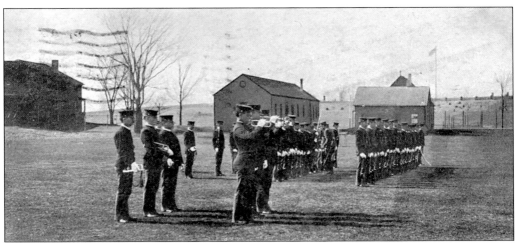

Fort Hamilton was established in 1825 to serve as part of the New York Harbor defense system, along with nearby Fort Lafayette and Fort Wadsworth, across the Narrows in Staten Island. This scene shows a drill in progress at Fort Hamilton, *c.* 1911 (Phillip and Loretta Stock.)

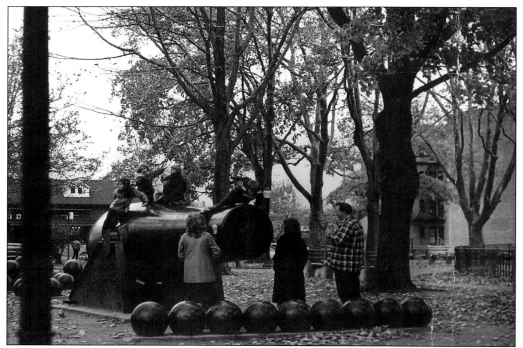

John Paul Jones Park is more familiarly known as "Cannonball Park." In this 1970s photograph, children and adults play on the 1865 Rodman gun, which was moved closer to 101st Street during the construction of the Verrazano Bridge. To the left is the original Hamilton House restaurant, which served excellent meals through the mid-1980s. (George Paszkewicz.)

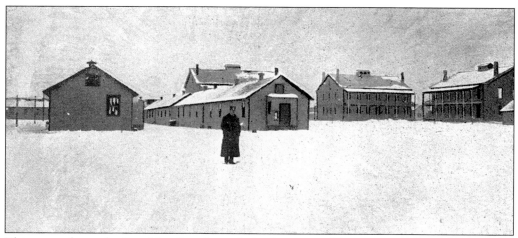

This scene shows the Fort Hamilton barracks in the winter. The site was once a Nyack Indian village. (Peter Syrdahl.)

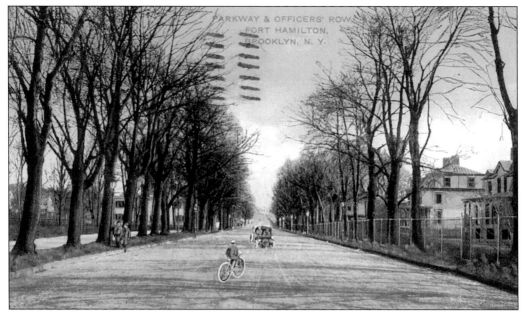

This scene shows the Parkway and Officers Row. With the construction of the Verrazano Bridge ramp, the houses were torn down and the street was narrowed. The Fort Hamilton Senior Citizens Center now stands where the houses were. (Ed Milanese.)

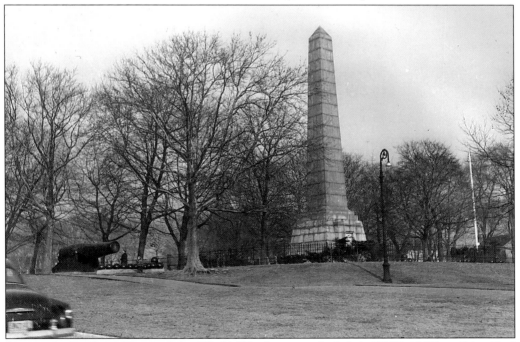

Here is the Rodman Gun and the World War I memorial obelisk (1917–1918) in John Paul Jones Park (4th Avenue and Shore Road) in 1952. The monument, cannon, and the Belt Parkway ramps in the foreground were moved during the construction of the Verrazano Bridge (1957–1964). (Bay Ridge Historical Society.)

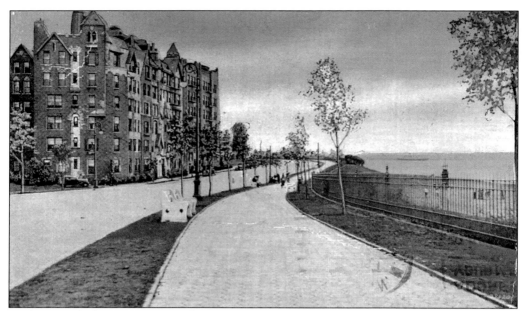

Looking south from 71st Street, this *c.* 1936 view shows Shore Road before the Belt Parkway was constructed. The Narrows Botanical Garden is now located at the right of the picture. (Phillip and Loretta Stock.)

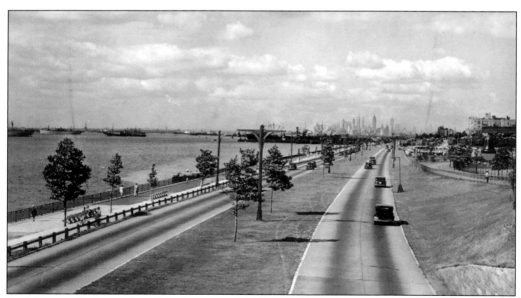

Looking north from the 80th Street pedestrian bridge, this *c.* 1940 view shows the Belt Parkway. (Phillip and Loretta Stock.)

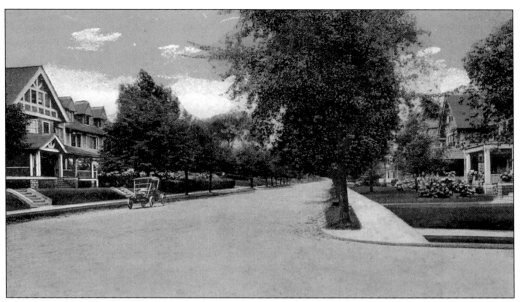

This view of Ridge Boulevard was taken looking east from 82nd Street in 1915. Many of these homes are still standing. (Peter Syrdahl.)

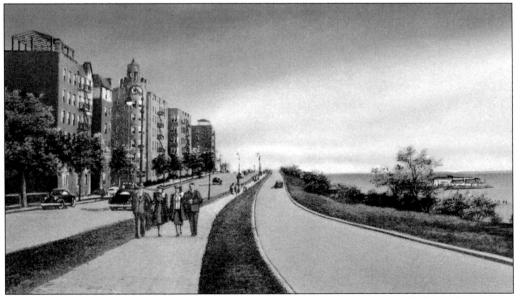

This view of Shore Drive was taken in the 1930s, before construction of the Belt Parkway was begun. It shows the transition from single-family homes to urban apartment living. (Peter Syrdahl.)

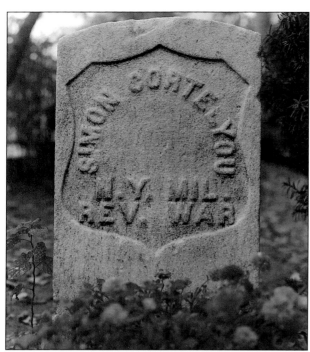

The remains of Simon Cortelyou (1746–1828) are interred in the Barkaloo Cemetery, located behind Xaverian High School, at McKay Place and Narrows Avenue. Below the name, the tombstone reads "N.Y. Mil. Rev. War."

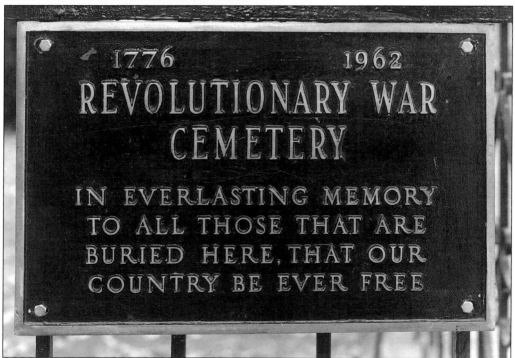

This plaque is located in the Barkaloo Cemetery, at Narrows Avenue and McKay Place. The cemetery is maintained by the Bay Ridge Historical Society in recognition of the early families of the area. (Bay Ridge Historical Society.)

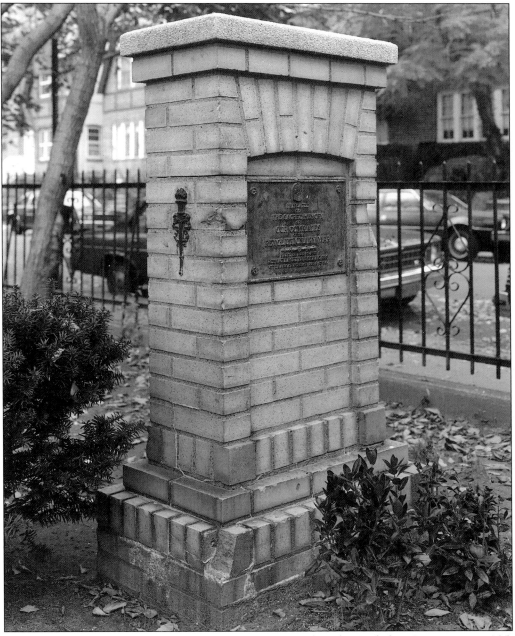

This memorial to the American Revolution was erected at the Barkaloo Cemetery in 1935. Prominent among the Barkaloo and other old Bay Ridge family members buried here are Revolutionary War participants Jacques Barkaloo and Simon Cortelyou.

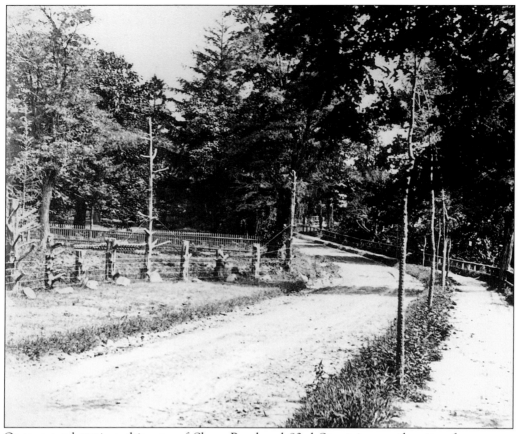

Once a rural setting, this area of Shore Road and 93rd Street is now the site of numerous apartment houses. (Samuel Winter Thomas.)

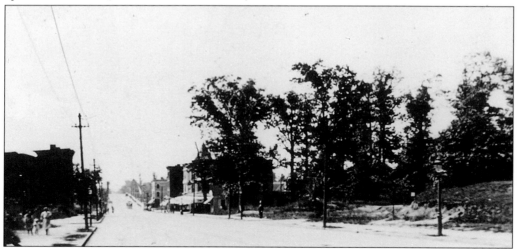

This view was taken looking south on 3rd Avenue from 75th Street (now Bay Ridge Parkway) c. 1901. Commercial enterprises are now located along this formerly tree-lined avenue. (Samuel Winter Thomas.)

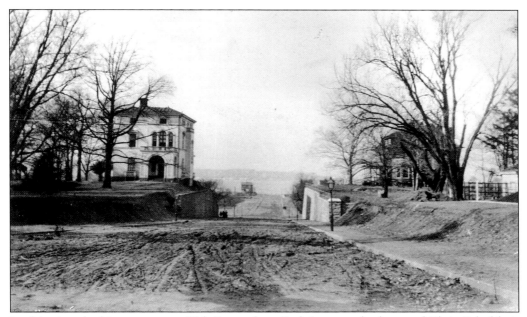

In this view, looking west on a 75th Street from 2nd Avenue, the home of Chris Schultheis (also known as "the Ridge") is on the right. The home of William Thomas, older brother of the photographer Samuel Winter Thomas, is on the left. That property was cut in half to make way for 75th Street and was torn down in 1927.

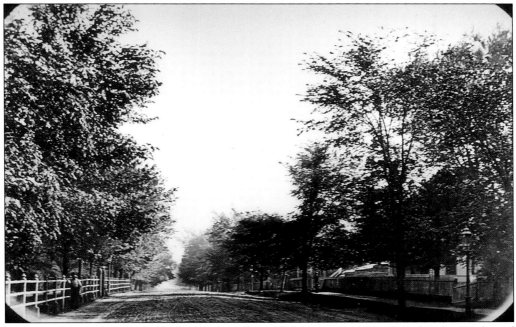

This is a view looking north on 2nd Avenue from 75th Street in 1893. Called Ridge Boulevard today, the street is one where apartment buildings predominate. (Samuel Winter Thomas.)

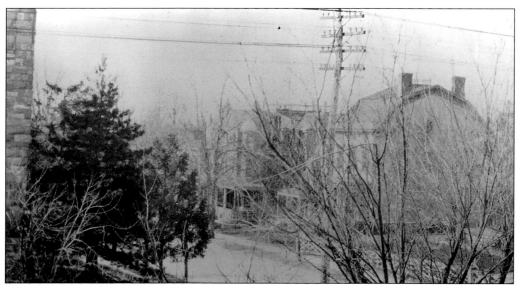

This view was taken looking west on Ovington Avenue from the O. Heinigke house at 4th Avenue on April 3, 1905. Bay Ridge Methodist Church is on the left.

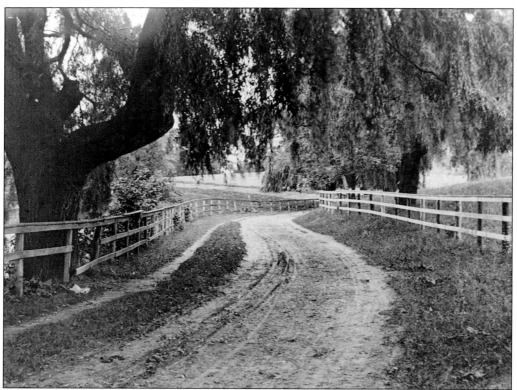

This scene shows Serpentine Road, now 67th Street, near 3rd Avenue. The rural aspect soon gave way to make room for private homes. (Samuel Winter Thomas.)

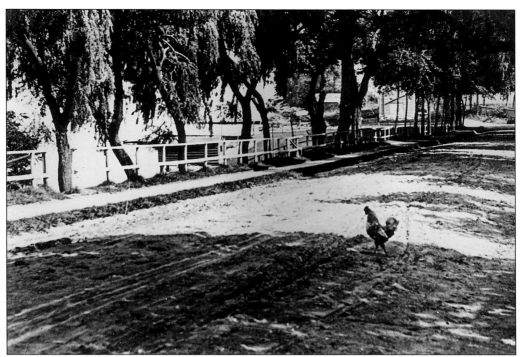

Even a proverbial "chicken crossing the road" was captured for posterity by Samuel Winter Thomas, at 79th Street and Shore Road.

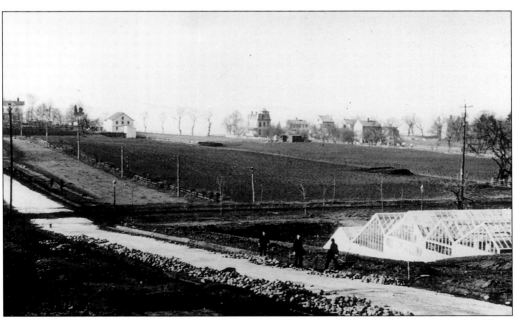

On 73rd Street near 1st Avenue, greenhouses stand in the back of where present-day Flagg Court is located. (Samuel Winter Thomas.)

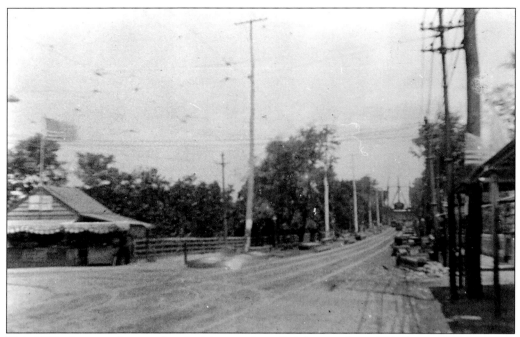

This 1892 photograph was taken looking north on 3rd Avenue from 65th Street. The structure for the new elevated railroad approached Bay Ridge, and the line, a branch of the 5th Avenue Elevated, opened in 1893. (Samuel Winter Thomas.)

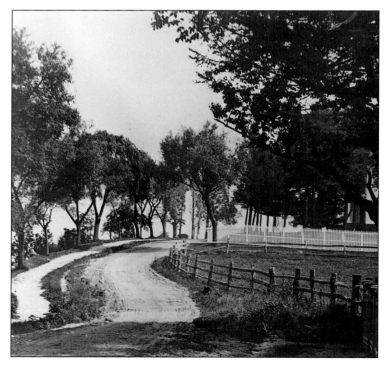

This view shows Shore Road and 72nd Street. The site of the present-day Xaverian High School is located a short carriage ride away. (Samuel Winter Thomas.)

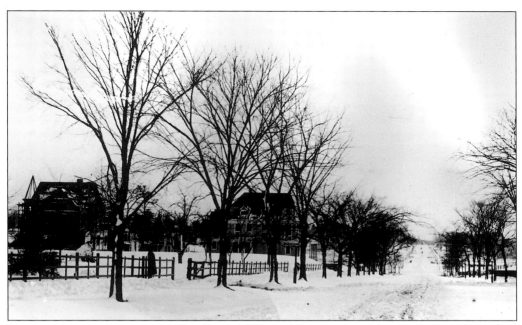

On a snowy day in January 1894, Samuel Winter Thomas aimed his camera south on 2nd Avenue (Ridge Boulevard) from 75th Street (Bay Ridge Parkway).

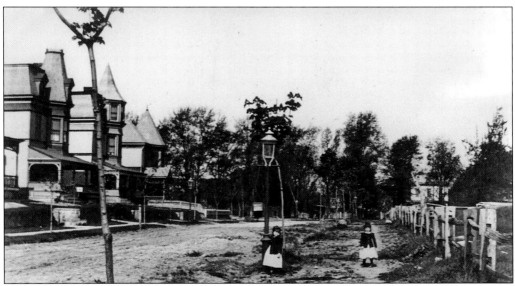

The Convent of Our Lady of Angels Church is now at this site, 73rd Street west from 4th Avenue, shown here in 1893. (Samuel Winter Thomas.)

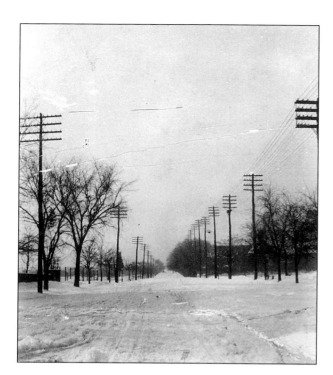

In the early 1900s, this view was taken looking south from Ovington Avenue along snowy 4th Avenue. (Samuel Winter Thomas.)

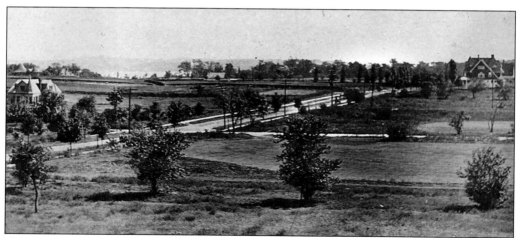

This view was taken looking south from 77th Street between 1st and 2nd Avenues in 1904, before the building boom dramatically altered the landscape. (Samuel Winter Thomas.)

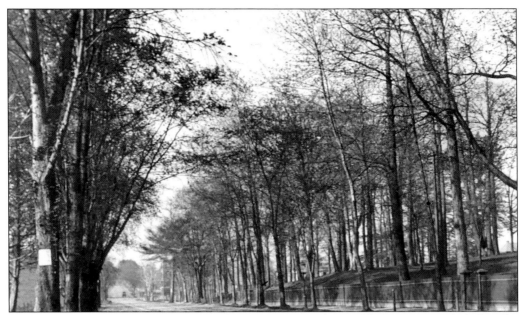

This photograph was taken looking south on 3rd Avenue from 75th Street in 1893, before the elm trees gave way to commercial enterprises. (Samuel Winter Thomas.)

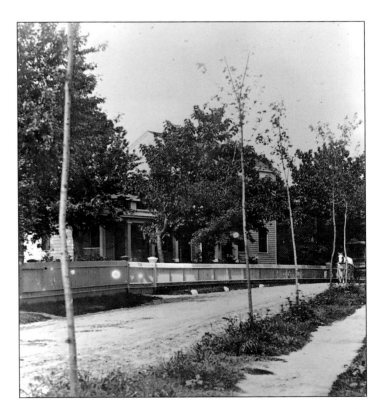

A horse-drawn wagon passes the residence of Henry MacKay (1846–1939), on Shore Road at 73rd Street in 1890. (Samuel Winter Thomas.)

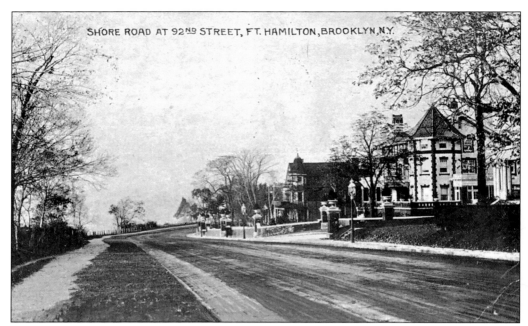

This postcard shows Shore Road at 92nd Street *c.* 1912. This area offered a spectacular view of the harbor—a view that is still enjoyed by the local residents. (Phillip and Loretta Stock.)

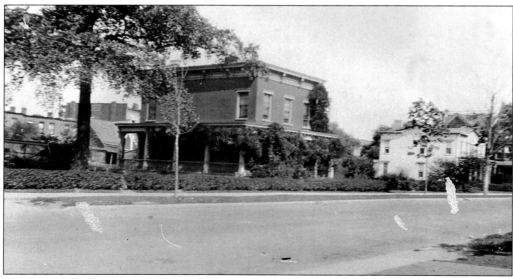

The north side of Ovington Avenue between 3rd and 4th Avenues is seen here in the early 1900s. (Bay Ridge Historical Society.)

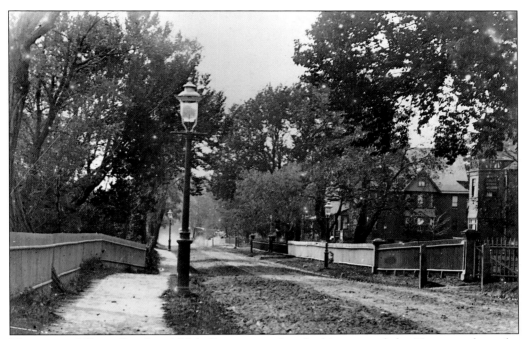

This view of Shore Road and 95th Street was taken looking toward the Narrows where the landmark Farrell house once stood. (Samuel Winter Thomas.)

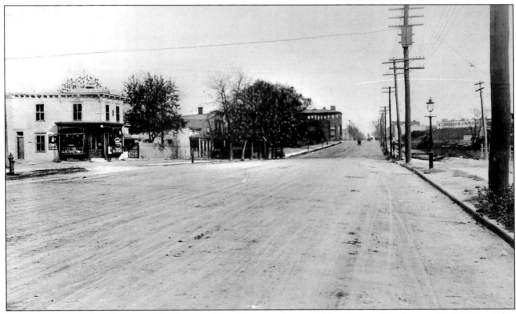

This early 1900s photograph shows 4th Avenue from 65th Street in the early 1900s. The elevated Gowanus Expressway covers this area today. (Samuel Winter Thomas.)

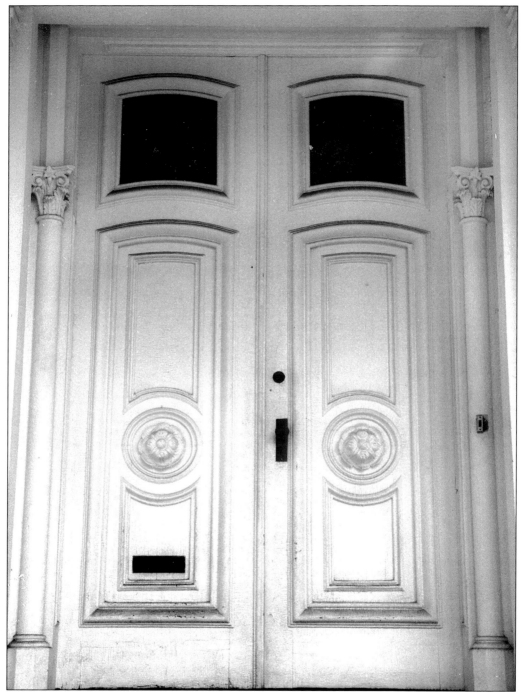

This shows the entrance door to the Farrell house. Behind the door of this landmark building lie several hoped-for adaptive reuses. Several community groups have come up with ideas and plans to use the building. However, these plans have yet to be realized due to a lack of funding. (Peter Syrdahl.)

Three

LIVING IN BAY RIDGE: STREETS, SCHOOLS, CHURCHES, AND ORGANIZATIONS

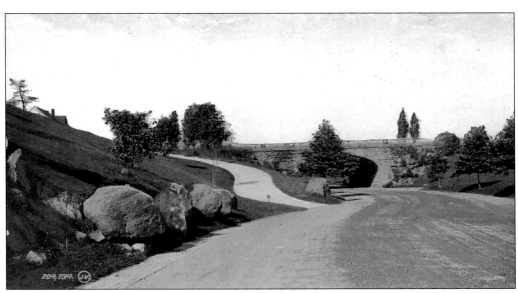

A postcard captures Shore Road Drive and 2nd Avenue in the early 1900s. (Ed Milanese.)

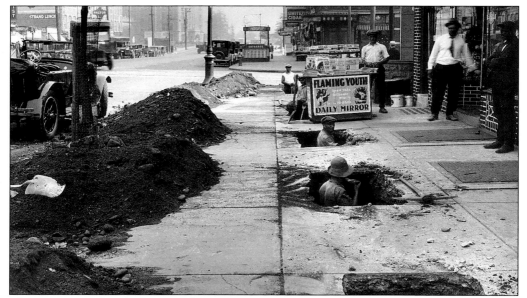

This view was taken looking north on the east side of 4th Avenue toward Bay Ridge Avenue on July 21, 1924. Sewer work proceeds beneath the well-stocked newsstand. The *New York Daily Mirror*, a Hearst morning newspaper, is in its first year of publication. The original subway entrances date from 1916, and the all-girls Bay Ridge High School stands in the distance. Note the touring car parked on the left. (Rutter, from Dr. Palisi.)

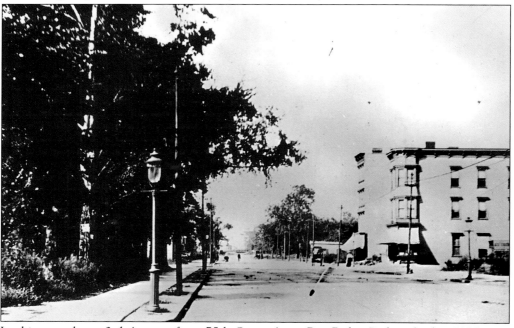

Looking north on 3rd Avenue from 75th Street (now Bay Ridge Parkway), this 1905 view shows that the big city is approaching: the paved avenue has sidewalks, and the houses and stores at 74th Street, on the right, indicate the advance of commerce onto 3rd Avenue. (Samuel Winter Thomas.)

This political handbill is from the campaign of William E. Cleary, who served Bay Ridge as Democratic congressman from World War I until 1932. (Courtesy of Dr. Jack Gabel.)

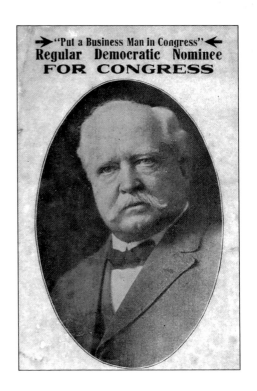

→ "Put a Business Man in Congress" ←
Regular Democratic Nominee
FOR CONGRESS

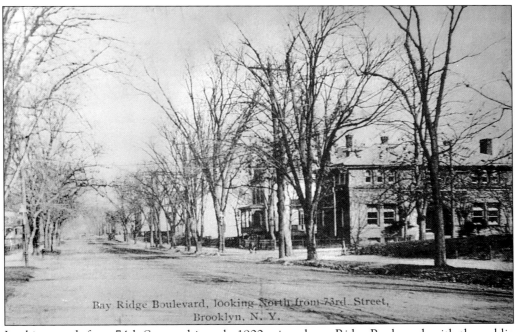

Bay Ridge Boulevard, looking North from 73rd Street, Brooklyn, N. Y.

Looking north from 74th Street, this early-1900s view shows Ridge Boulevard, with the public library on the right, on 73rd Street.

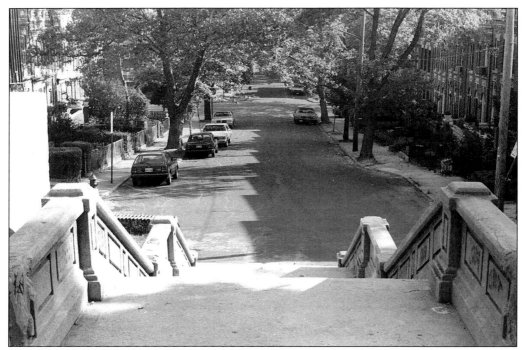

A staircase leads from Ridge Boulevard to Colonial Road on 74th Street.

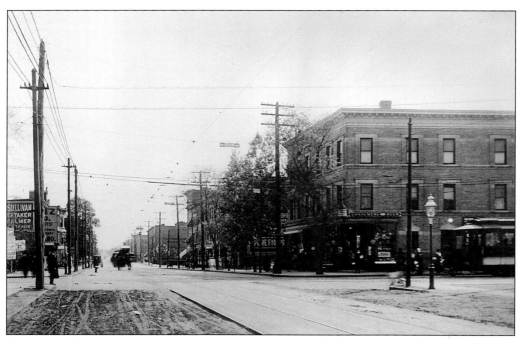

This June 1914 photograph shows Bay Ridge Avenue and 5th Avenue, with a trolley on the right, where a B1 bus stop is currently located. It was taken looking south from the street in front of what is now the Alpine Theater.

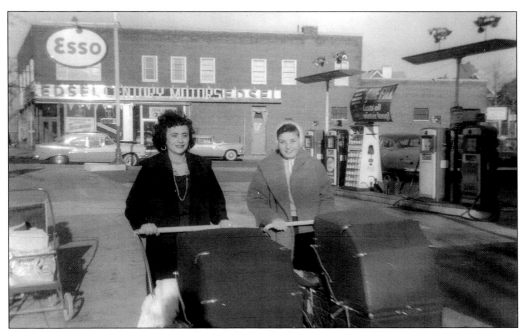

In January 1958, a pair of new mothers took their babies (in carriages) for a ride on 4th Avenue. In the background, near Senator Street, are an Esso gas station and a Ford Edsel auto showroom. (George Manos.)

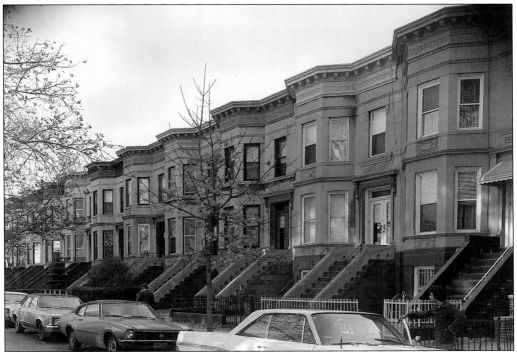

These are typical Bay Ridge row houses, located at Ovington Avenue between 3rd and 4th Avenues.

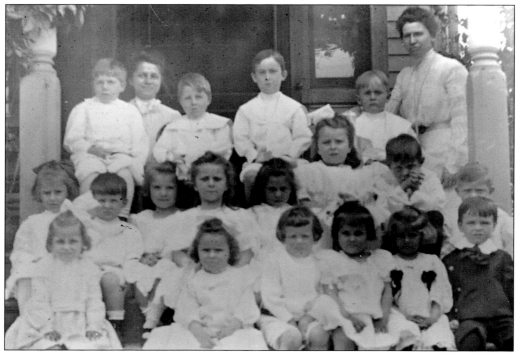

Miss Dunne of Bay Ridge is seen with her kindergarten class in June 1904. (Samuel Winter Thomas.)

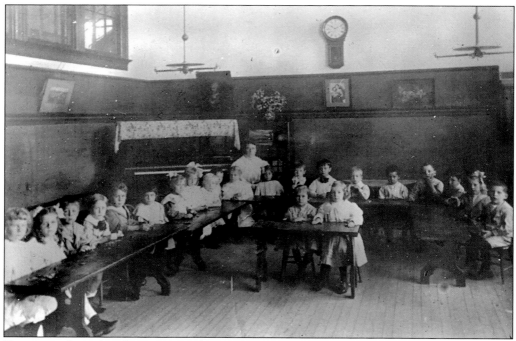

Youngsters from days long gone make up this 1909 classroom scene in Public School 102K. (Samuel Winter Thomas.)

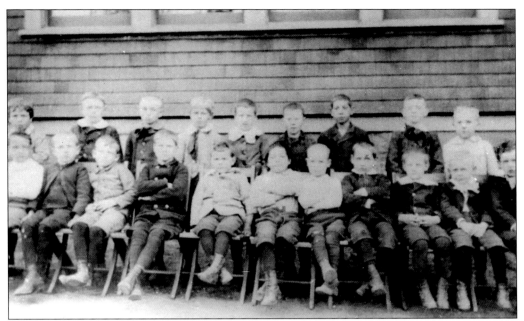

This was the first class (1891–1892) of Public School 102, located at 71st Street and Ridge Boulevard. (Courtesy of PS 102K.)

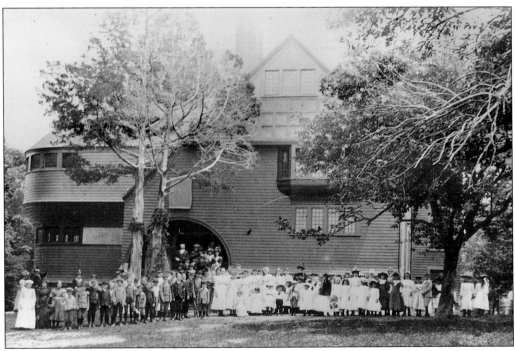

District School No. 2, on 71st Street between 2nd and 3rd Avenue, was built in 1883 to replace the old schoolhouse on 3rd Avenue. On June 30, 1893, the students and faculty posed for Samuel Winter Thomas. The brick Public School 102K superseded this wood building in 1904.

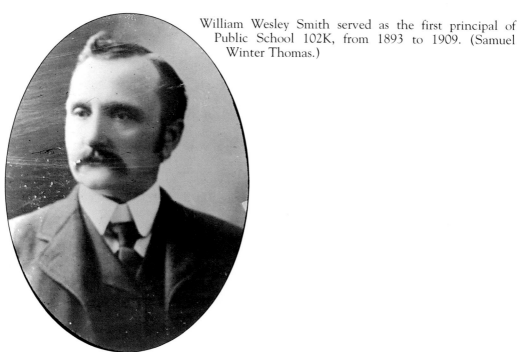

William Wesley Smith served as the first principal of Public School 102K, from 1893 to 1909. (Samuel Winter Thomas.)

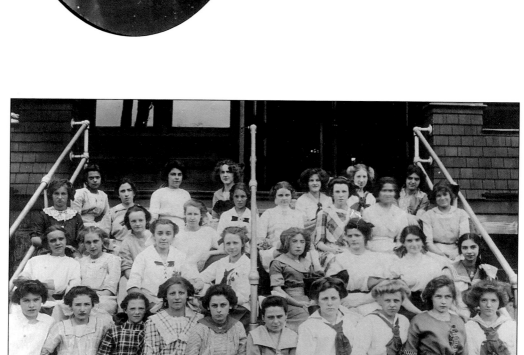

This undated photograph shows members of the upper-grade class of Public School 102. (Courtesy of PS 102K.)

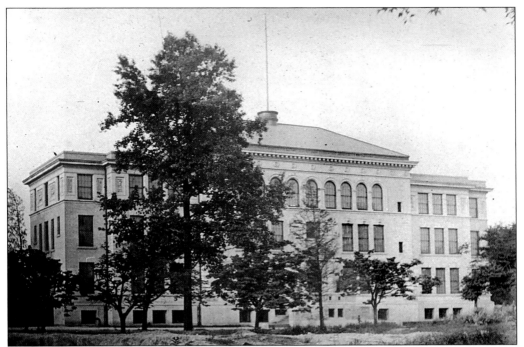

Samuel Winter Thomas took this view of the soon-to-open Public School 102 at 71st Street and 2nd Avenue in Brooklyn on August 30, 1904. This building replaced the old wooden New Utrecht District School No. 2 that stood to the left, in what is today the schoolyard.

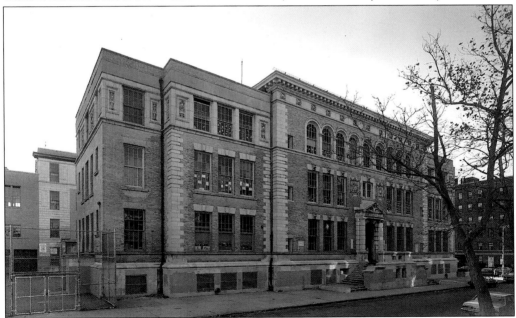

The Public School 102 building built in 1904 was connected to a new building at 72nd Street in 1930 to form one large school, providing prekindergarten to fifth grade classes to more than 1,200 ethnically diverse students. (Perlmutter, Bay Ridge Historical Society.)

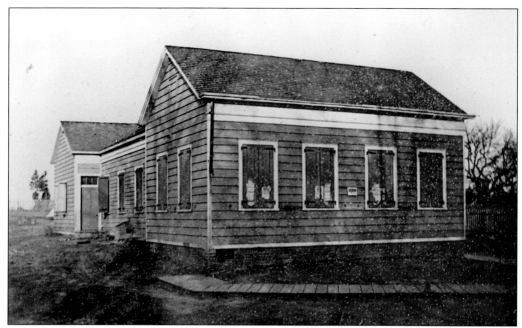

This little yellow schoolhouse stood on 3rd Avenue at 73rd Street in 1890. (Samuel Winter Thomas.)

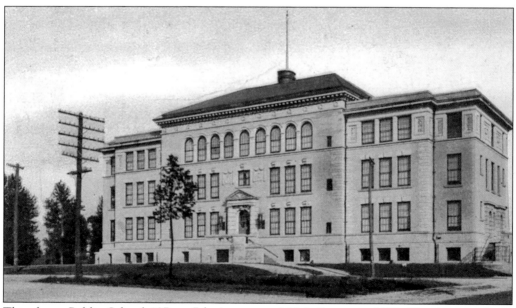

This shows Public School 127, at 7th Avenue and 79th Street, in 1909. The front yard was reduced in size in the 1960s to accommodate increased automobile traffic resulting from the creation of the Verrazano Bridge approach highway, which had sliced through and destroyed hundreds of homes in what was then the heavily residential eastern end of Bay Ridge. (Peter Syrdahl.)

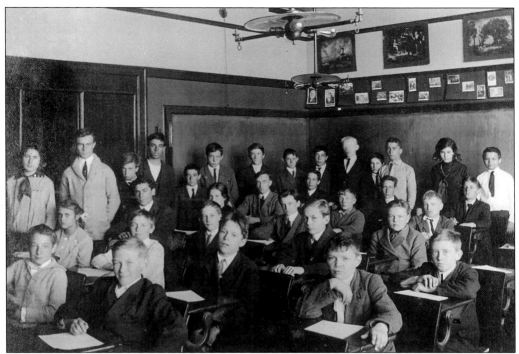

This photograph was taken in Public School 104K, at 5th Avenue and 92nd Street, in the early 1920s. The young woman standing second from the right in the back is Ida Betz, whose family once resided in Bay Ridge. (Courtesy of John Ryan.)

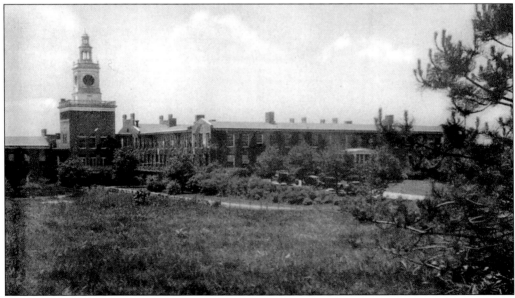

This is a 1920s view of Poly Prep Country Day School, at 7th Avenue near 92nd Street. The duck-filled lakes and rural setting of this otherwise advanced school is little changed from what it and Bay Ridge looked like in the early years of the last century. (Peter Syrdahl.)

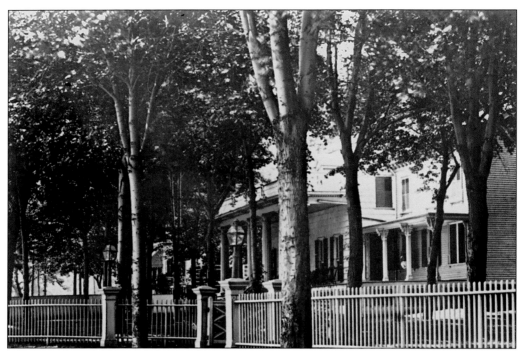

The Crescent Athletic Club, on Shore Road, had many clubhouses. Samuel Winter Thomas labeled this one the "Old Clubhouse."

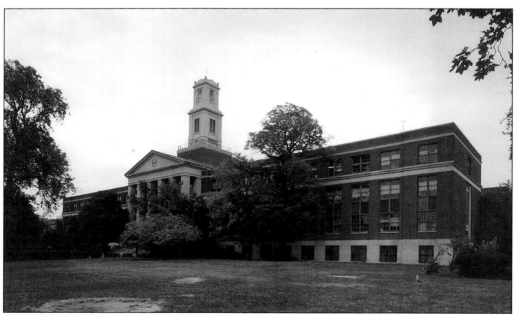

Fort Hamilton High School opened in 1941 on the grounds of the former Crescent Athletic Club.

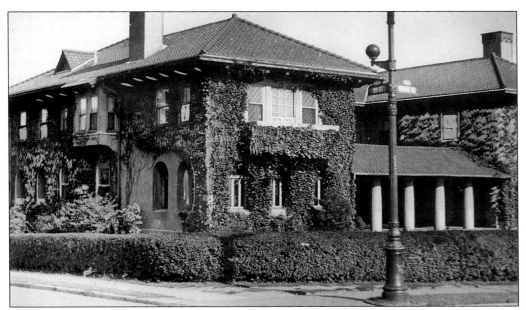

Fontbonne Hall, a private high school for girls, was a private residence when this photograph was taken in the 1930s. Located on Shore Road at 99th Street, it once served as "Diamond Jim" Brady and Lillian Russell's summer home. (Bay Ridge Historical Society.)

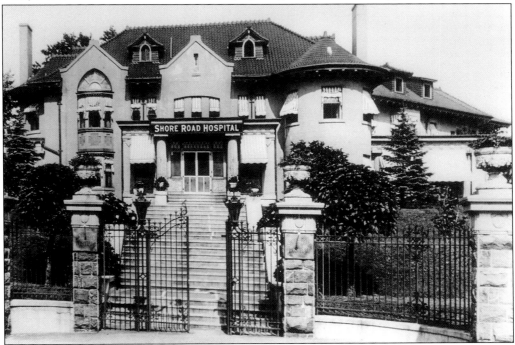

The Shore Road Hospital, at Shore Road and 91st Street, was a converted mansion. In the late 1960s, it was demolished and replaced by the Shore Hill Towers senior residence. The Bay Ridge Historical Society holds its monthly meetings in the community room at this site. (Peter Syrdahl.)

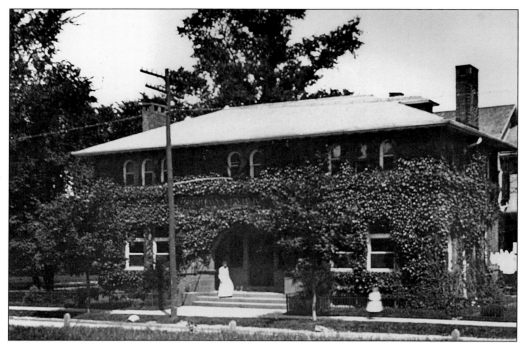

This photograph of Bay Ridge Library, at 73rd Street and Ridge Boulevard, was taken in August 1904. (Samuel Winter Thomas.)

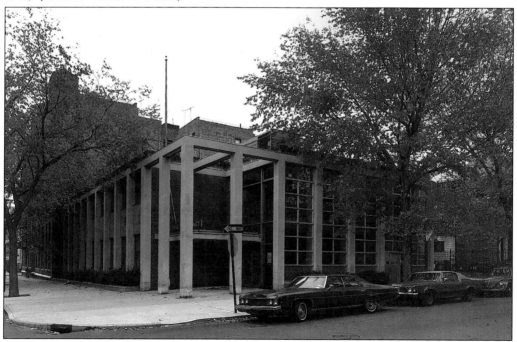

In 1959, the present Bay Ridge branch of the Brooklyn Public Library reopened at the same location, on the corner of Ridge Boulevard and 73rd Street. (Perlmutter, Bay Ridge Historical Society.)

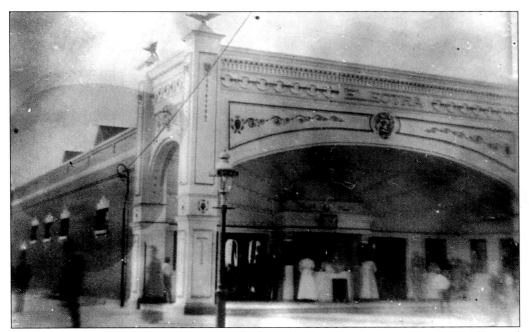

The Electra Theater is seen here as it looked shortly after it opened in 1910. (Samuel Winter Thomas.)

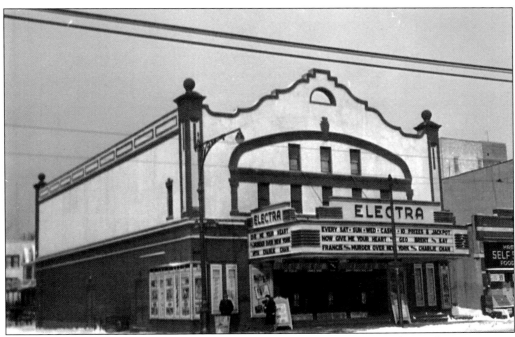

The Electra Theater, at the northwest corner of 3rd Avenue and Bay Ridge Parkway, is now a supermarket. This photograph was taken in 1941. (Courtesy of the NYC Municipal Archives.)

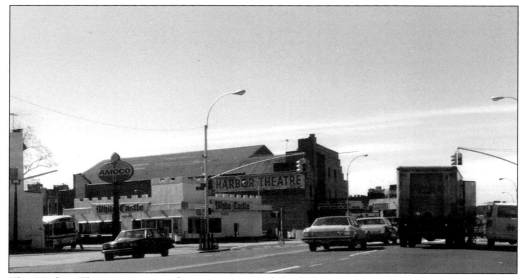

The Harbor Theatre is now a fitness center, and the White Castle restaurant and its parking lot are now an office building and another restaurant, at the corner of 4th Avenue and 92nd Street. (George Manos.)

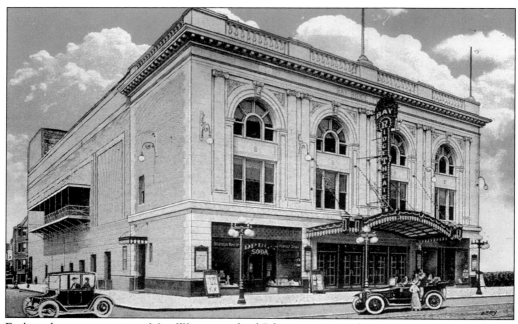

Early in her career, actress Mae West won the $5 first prize in a talent contest at the Bay Ridge Theatre, at 3rd Avenue and 72nd Street. This view dates from c. 1915. (Peter Syrdahl.)

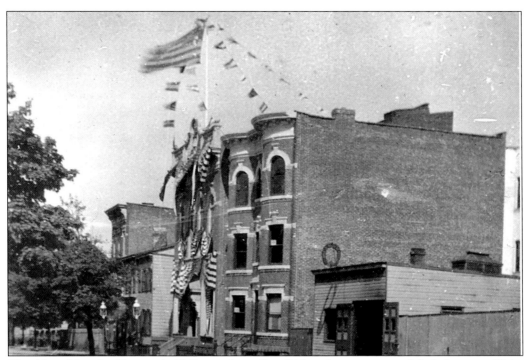

The New Utrecht Firemen's Hall stood on Bay Ridge Avenue west of 3rd Avenue. This photograph was taken in 1909. (Samuel Winter Thomas.)

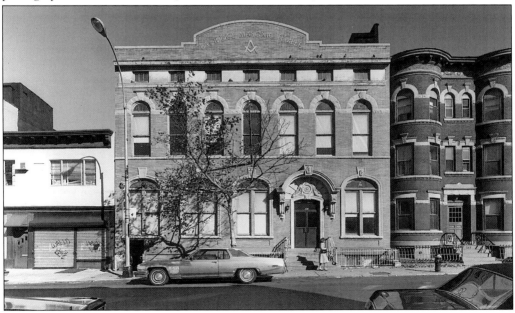

The New Utrecht Firemen's Hall was in use throughout most of the 20th century as a meeting hall for the Fraternal Order of Masons. It became a private school in the late 1990s. The names and shields of the firefighting units that were its first tenants can still be seen on the face of the building.

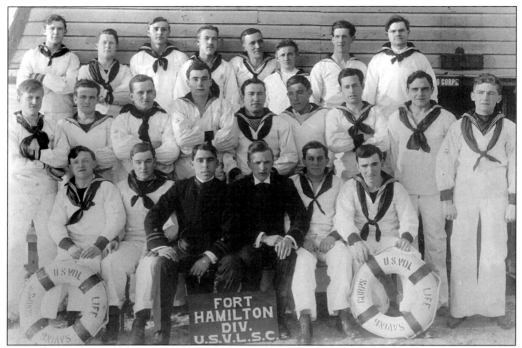

Members of the Fort Hamilton Division of the United States Volunteer Life Saving Corps pose for a picture. (Courtesy of John Ryan.)

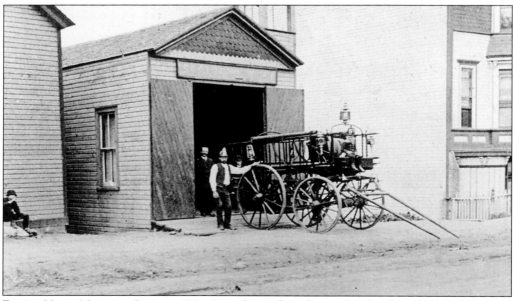

Engine House Neptune Company No. 2 was located on the south side of 67th Street below 3rd Avenue. (Samuel Winter Thomas.)

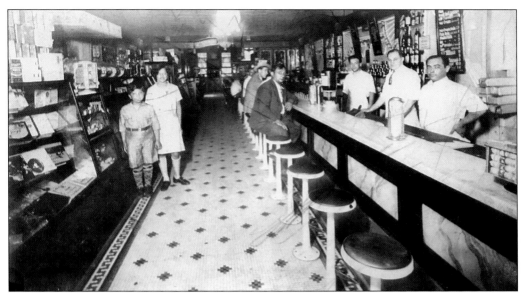

During the 1940s, this luncheonette was located on 4th Avenue. It also sold candy, at the counter on the left. Note the boy wearing knickers. (Courtesy of Sylvia Kramer.)

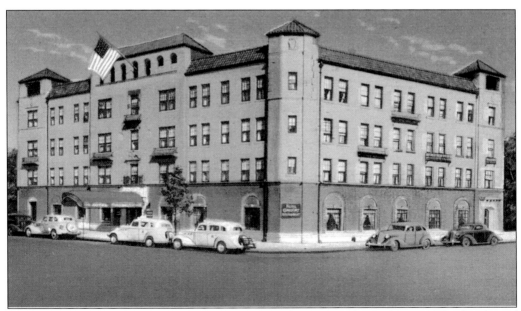

This c. 1940 view shows the Hotel Gregory, at 84th Street and 4th Avenue. The families of many post–World War II baby boomers celebrated various events in the first-floor banquet room of what is now a Comfort Inn. (Phillip and Loretta Stock.)

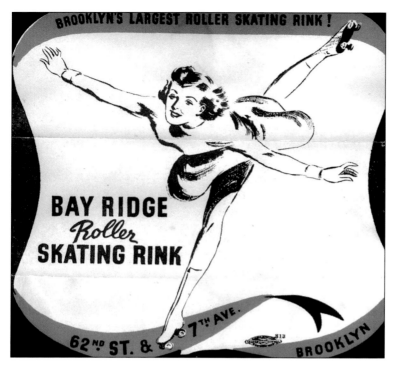

This is a c. 1940 advertisement for the Bay Ridge Roller Skating Rink. The rink was a favorite meeting place for the younger set. Many couples who met here established lasting relationships. (Courtesy of Charles Dono.)

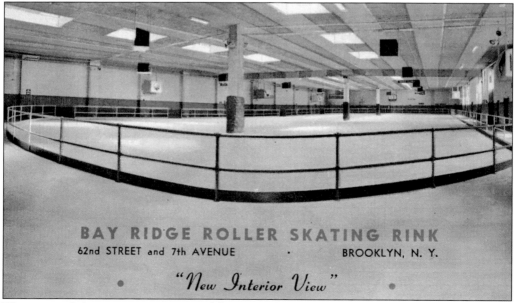

This postcard shows an interior view of the Bay Ridge Skating Rink, located at 62nd Street and 7th Avenue. It was always fun when the music stopped and everyone had to reverse direction. (Peter Syrdahl.)

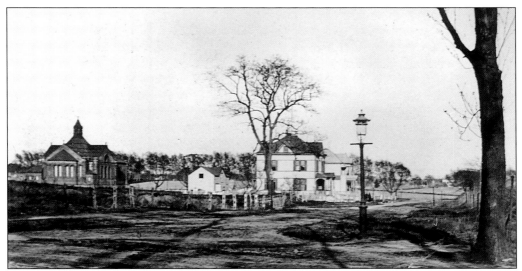

This early photograph was taken looking east from 75th Street (Bay Ridge Parkway) and 3rd Avenue in 1891. The newly constructed Our Lady of Angels Roman Catholic Church stands at 4th Avenue and 74th Street. Across from the church is a barn. The row of trees in the distance beyond the planted fields is on 6th Avenue. (Samuel Winter Thomas.)

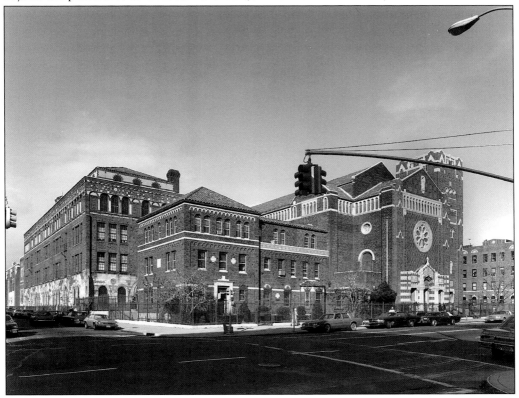

Our Lady of Angels Roman Catholic Church is seen here on 4th Avenue between 73rd and 74th Streets. (Perlmutter, Bay Ridge Historical Society.)

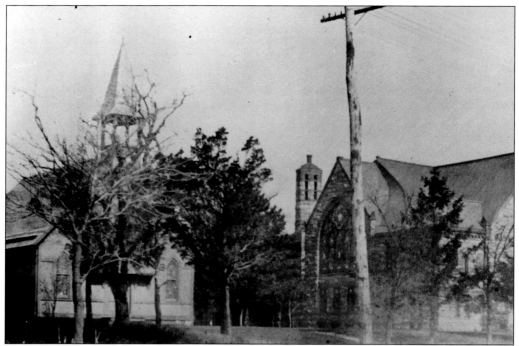

This is an early 1900s view of the west side of 4th Avenue between Ovington Avenue and 72nd Street. The Bay Ridge Methodist Church still stands on the right near Ovington Avenue. The chapel on the left was replaced by a school, which later became a day-care center. (Samuel Winter Thomas.)

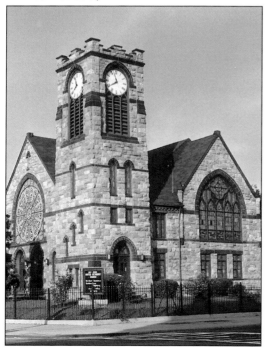

The Bay Ridge United Methodist Church, at 4th Avenue and Ovington Avenue, was built in 1899. (Rita Unz.)

Christ Church, at 67th Street and 3rd Avenue, was later moved to 4th Avenue and 75th Street (Bay Ridge Parkway), where it became Good Shepherd Lutheran Church. (Samuel Winter Thomas.)

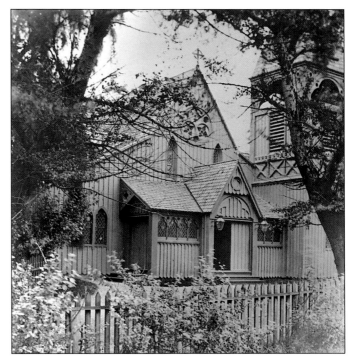

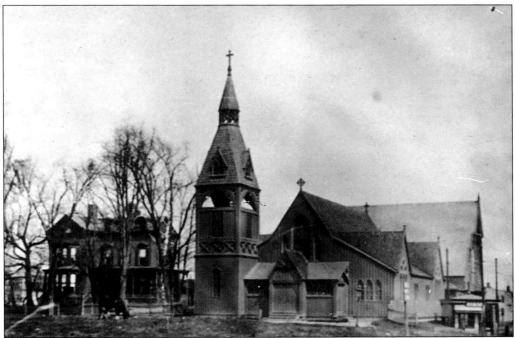

The Episcopal church at 3rd Avenue and 67th Street is shown c. 1900. The noise from the passing trolleys (see poles at the right) caused the congregation to sell the building. Moved to 4th Avenue and 75th Street, the building became Good Shepherd Lutheran Church. (Samuel Winter Thomas.)

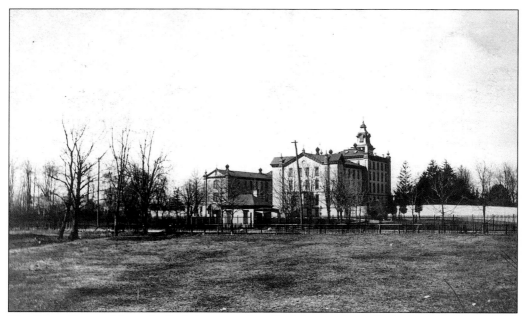

The Kings County Home for Inebriates stands at 2nd Avenue (now Ridge Boulevard) and 91st Street in the 1890s. (Samuel Winter Thomas.)

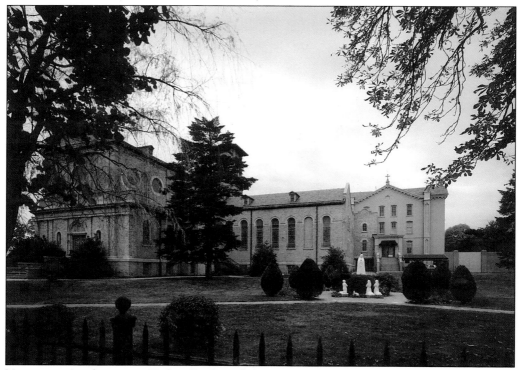

Visitation Academy, on Ridge Boulevard between 89th and 91st Streets, incorporated some of the buildings from the Kings County Home for Inebriates. (Perlmutter, Bay Ridge Historical Society.)

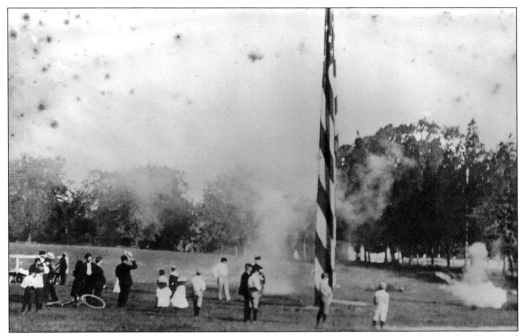

The morning salute of the 44-star flag in Bay Ridge on July 4, 1894, includes fireworks. (Samuel Winter Thomas.)

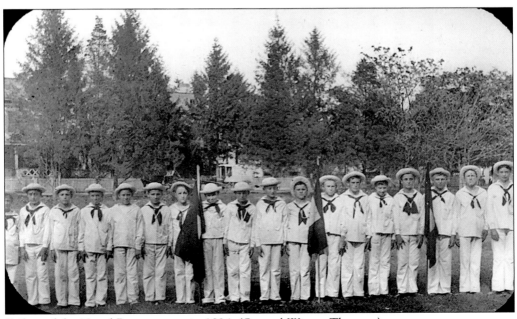

Sailors of the Naval Reserve pose in 1894. (Samuel Winter Thomas.)

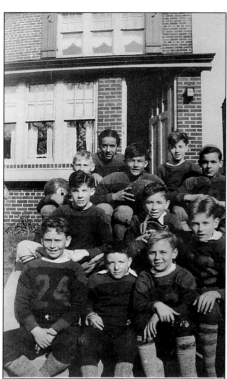

A football team poses on the stoop of 961 76th Street in December 1933. (Gerald Chabert collection, Tom Sarro Archives.)

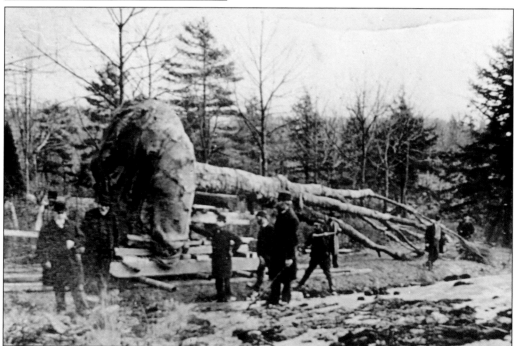

This Great Penn elm tree was removed from Fort Hamilton and delivered to Wilkes-Barre, Pennsylvania. (Samuel Winter Thomas.)

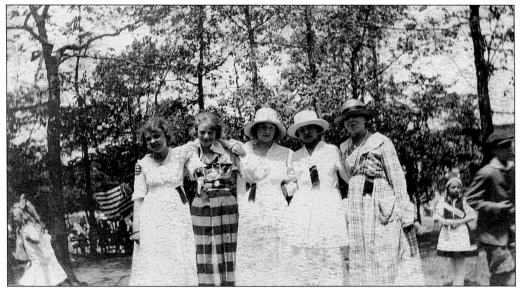

Five patriotic women celebrate in McKinley Park in July 1918. The woman second from the left is Ann Nielsen. (Courtesy of Doris Cruz.)

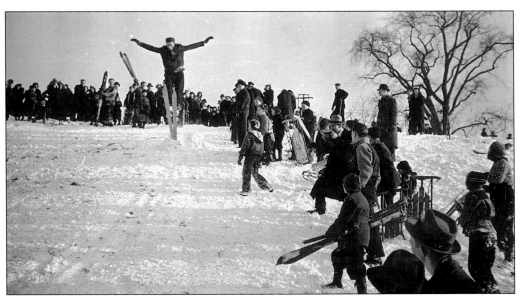

Bliss (Owl's Head) Park is a busy place in the winter of 1939. (Gerald Chabert collection, Tom Sarro Archives.)

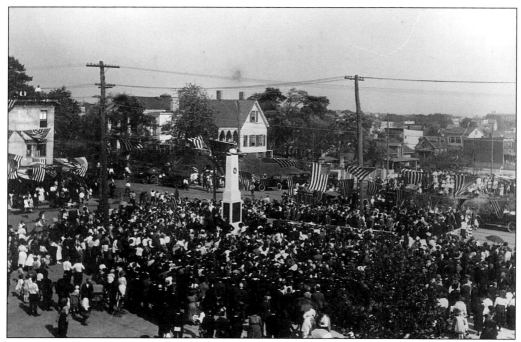

Shown is the dedication of the World War I memorial in 1920. This view was taken looking northeast from 4th Avenue between 94th and 95th Streets. (Courtesy of John Ryan.)

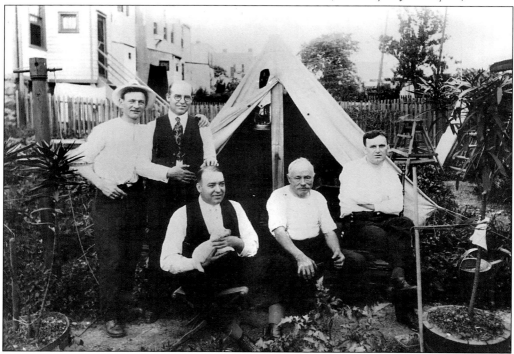

A family group poses in the rear yard of a house on 92nd Street c. World War I. (Courtesy of John Ryan.)

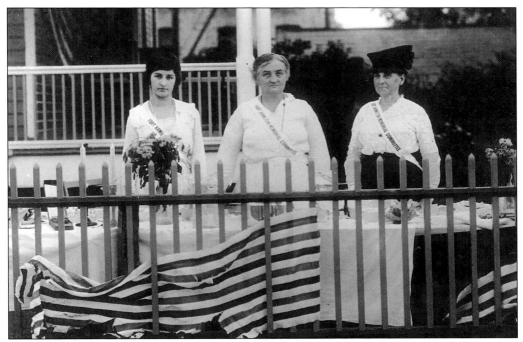

Members of the Ladies Committee raised funds for the World War I memorial, located at 4th Avenue and 95th Street. On the left is Marguerite Betz, a member of the Monument Committee (Courtesy of John Ryan.)

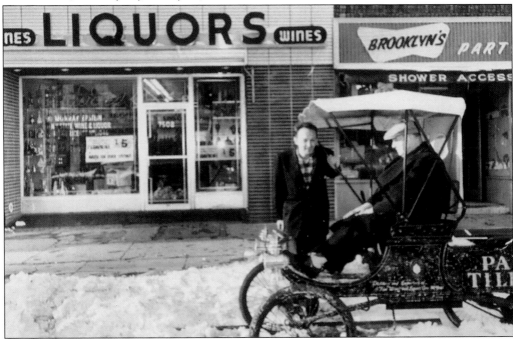

Murray Epstein (left), the owner of the liquor store on 13th Avenue at Bay Ridge Parkway, and Hyman Hameroff (right) admire an old time car in 1951. (Courtesy of Sylvia Kramer.)

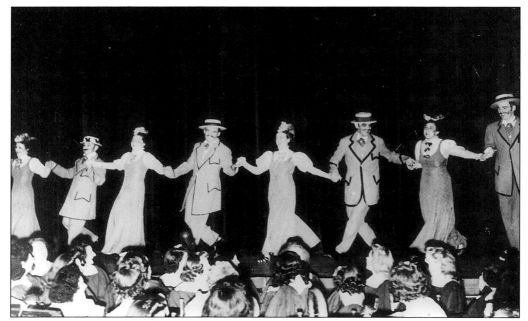

At Bay Ridge High School, "Faculty Fun," or "Buy-A-Bomber-Drive," is staged in May 1943. This school was for girls only until the 1980s, when it became the coeducational High School of Telecommunications Arts and Technology. (Courtesy of Louise Colavito.)

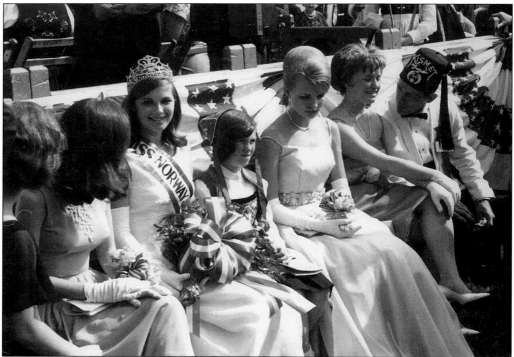

The crowned Miss Norway and friends are seen at the reviewing stand at the Norwegian Constitution Day Parade in the 1960s. (George Paszkewicz.)

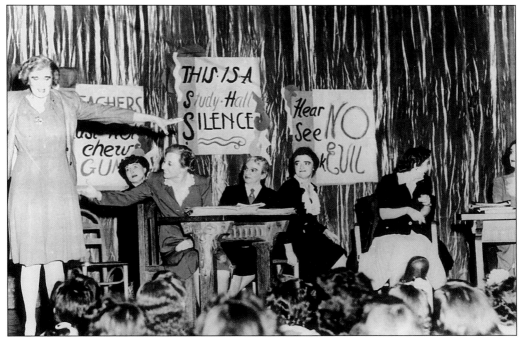

In May 1943, teachers and students perform in a "Faculty Fun" show at the Bay Ridge High School to raise money for World War II war bonds. (Louise Colavito.)

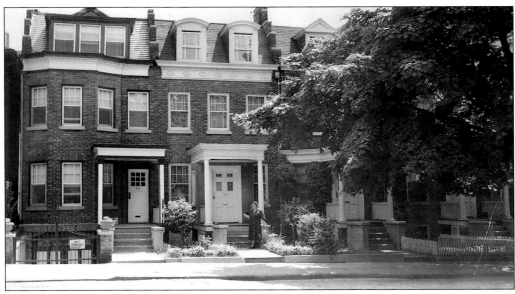

George Paszkewicz's mother stands in front of her row house home, at 174 71st Street, on June 6, 1961.

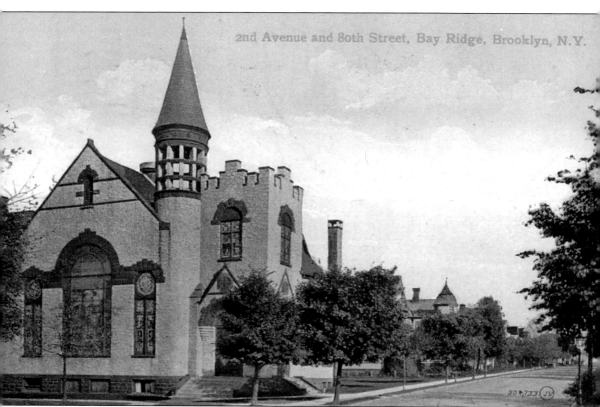

This c. 1908 postcard shows Union Church, on 2nd Avenue (Ridge Boulevard) and 80th Street. Union Church was the result of the merger of the Bay Ridge Presbyterian Church and the Bay Ridge Reformed (Dutch) Church. The building contains some stained glass windows from the Tiffany Studio. (Phillip and Loretta Stock.)

Four

GETTING AROUND IN BAY RIDGE: TRANSPORTATION OLD AND NEW

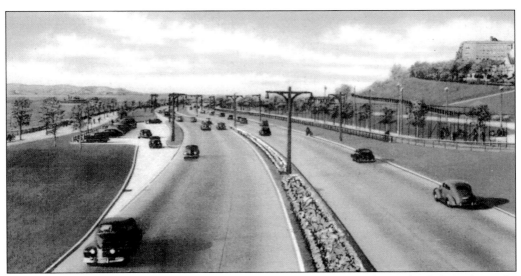

This view, looking north from the 4th Avenue overpass c. 1940, shows the Belt Parkway. In the 1970s, the section of road around Bay Ridge was also named Leif Ericsson Drive. In the late 1990s, the entire parkway was also named the POW/MIA Memorial Highway. (Phillip and Loretta Stock.)

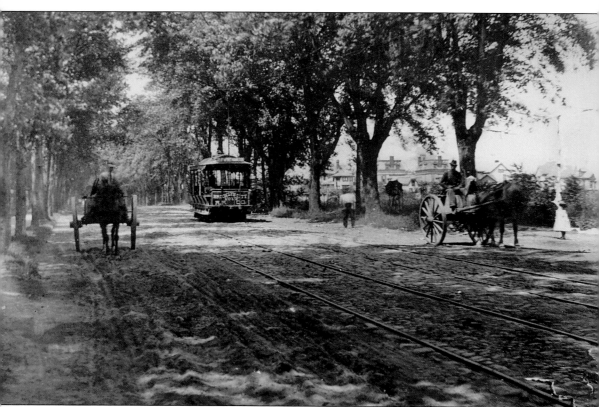

The new electric trolley, which replaced the steam-powered train, heads north on 3rd Avenue from 75th Street in the 1890s, while the horse-drawn carts stick to the unpaved part of the avenue. (Samuel Winter Thomas.)

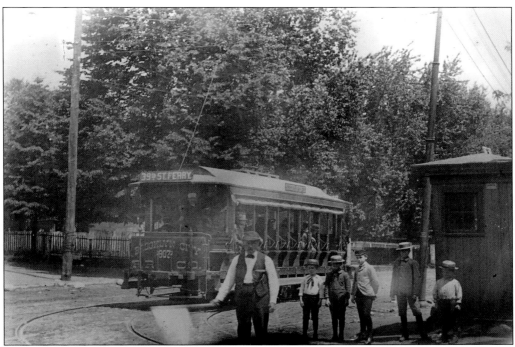

Trolley No. 809 of the Brooklyn City Railroad Company stands at 3rd Avenue and Bay Ridge Avenue (69th Street). The car ran by way of 2nd Avenue to the 39th Street ferry. (Samuel Winter Thomas.)

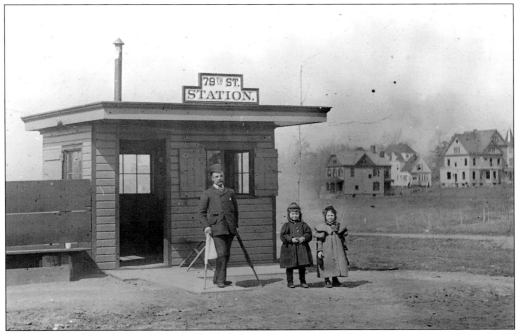

A flagman and two girls wait at the 79th Street station of the 3rd Avenue trolley on March 17, 1894. (Samuel Winter Thomas.)

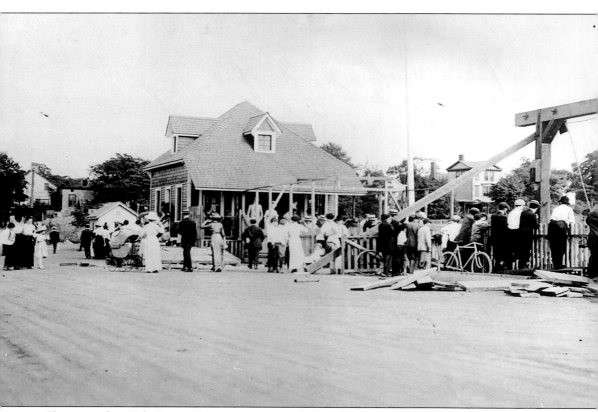

Shown is the 69th Street Pier on a summer day in the early 1900s. Note the bicycles, the lady with the baby carriage, and the men in their derbies, straw hats, and caps. (Bay Ridge Historical Society.)

This ferry schedule to Bay Ridge dates from 1874. (Samuel Winter Thomas.)

SUMMER ARRANGEMENT.

Commencing June 1, 1874.

THE

BAY RIDGE
FERRY BOAT

LEAVES BAY RIDGE.	LEAVES Wall Street Ferry, N. Y.
8.00 A. M.	8.30 A. M.
9.10 "	11.00 "
12.45 P. M.	2.00 P.M.
2.35 "	4.00 "
4.35 "	5.15 "
5.50 "	6.30 "

FARE, FIFTEEN CENTS.

Children between the ages of 3 and 12 Years, 8 Cents. Children going to and from School, 5 Cents.
TO BE PAID ON THE BOAT.

☞ Passengers to Bay Ridge having to pass through the same gates at the Wall St. Ferry as the Brooklyn Passengers, [there being no other entrance.] must also pay, on entering, the usual Brooklyn Ferriage.

THE BOAT WILL NOT RUN ON SUNDAYS.

Bergner Amateur Press

EPISODES
In the
HISTORY OF BAY RIDGE

OUR NEW FERRY-BOAT.

Who built it.
Why we built it.
How we built it.
Where we built it.
What we did with it.

INCIDENTAL SKETCH OF THE ATHENEUM.

BAY RIDGE,
PAST, PRESENT AND FUTURE

AT THE

SUNDAY SCHOOL ROOM
OF CHRIST CHURCH.
THIRD AVENUE, BAY RIDGE.

Thursday Evening, October 3, 1889 at 8 O'clock.

MR. SAMUEL W. THOMAS

Will distribute some "Chestnuts" gathered twenty years ago.

Admission 25 Cents,—Reserved Seats, 50 Cents.

TICKETS CAN BE OBTAINED AT THE POST-OFFICE.

The history of Bay Ridge was the subject of this broadside from October 1889. Samuel Winter Thomas participated at the event held in the Atheneum, at 2nd Avenue and 70th Street. (Samuel Winter Thomas.)

113

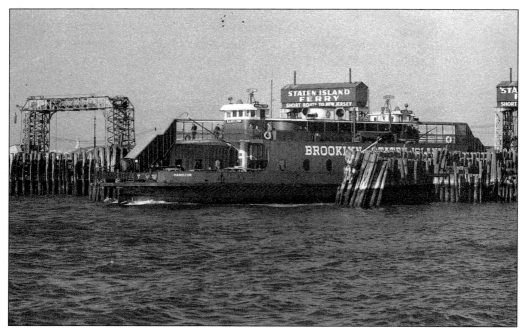

The Brooklyn–Staten Island ferryboat *Hamilton* is seen here at the 69th Street Pier *c.* 1961. This private ferry service discontinued operations within a week after the Verrazano Bridge opened in November 1964. (George Paszkewicz.)

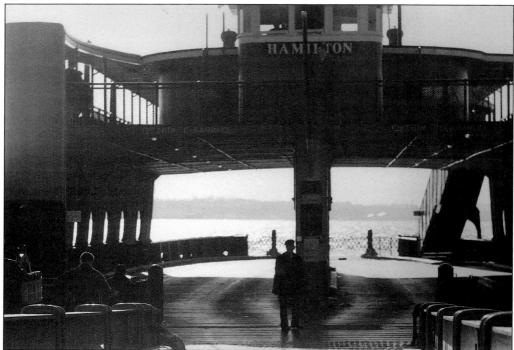

This was a driver's view of the ferryboat *Hamilton* at the 69th Street Pier. The boat ride to Staten Island, in the background, took 15 minutes. (George Paszkewicz.)

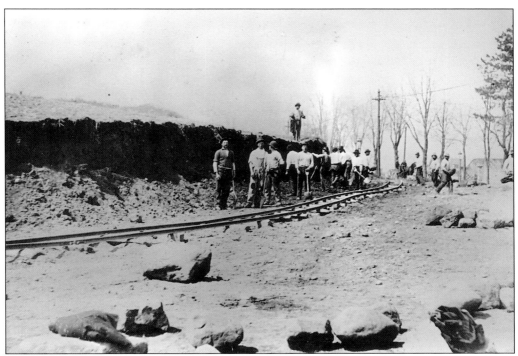

Workmen built this railway to haul away earth as they leveled a hill on 3rd Avenue between 82nd and 84th Street in 1896. (Samuel Winter Thomas.)

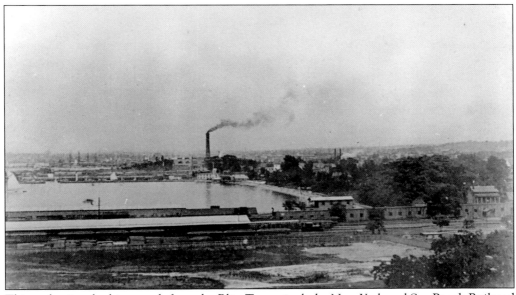

This early view, looking north from the Bliss Tower, includes New York and Sea Beach Railroad trains in the yard in the middle foreground. The Brooklyn Army Terminal was later built on the adjoining shore. The smokestack signifies the burgeoning industrial waterfront of Brooklyn. (Samuel Winter Thomas.)

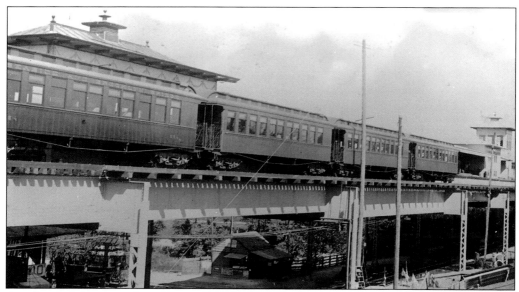

An elevated train stands in the new 65th Street station at 3rd Avenue on October 2, 1893. Service on the line ended in June 1940, and part of the structure was incorporated into the Gowanus Parkway. (Samuel Winter Thomas.)

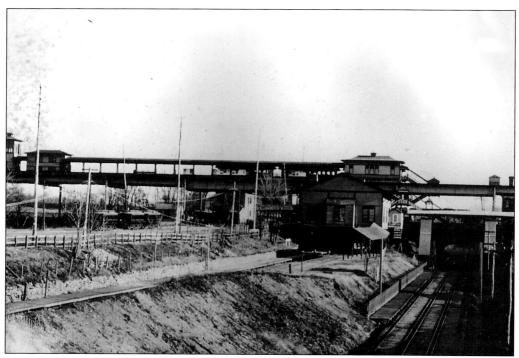

Looking east from 2nd Avenue and 65th Street on January 19, 1894, Samuel Winter Thomas's camera captures the Long Island Railroad and station on the right, the year-old elevated railroad station above 3rd Avenue at 65th Street, and the trolleys gathering on 65th Street on the left.

The 4th Avenue Brooklyn Subway opened to 86th Street in January 1916. It was extended to 95th Street in October 1925. (Peter Syrdahl.)

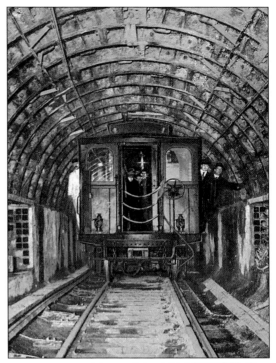

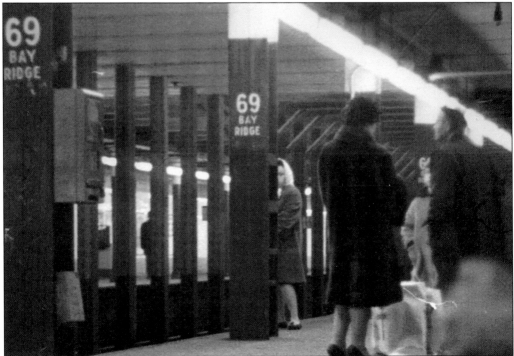

Shown is the platform of the Bay Ridge Avenue (69th Street) subway station in the early 1960s. The original 1916 tile work was covered over by new tiles in the 1970s. (George Paszkewicz.)

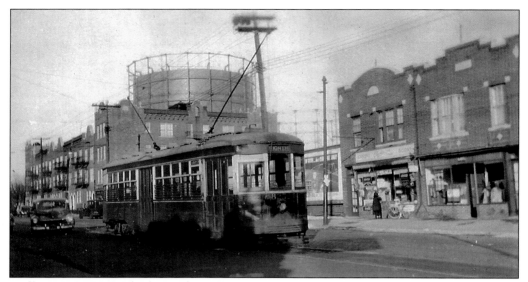

Trolley No. 8252 travels along 8th Avenue just north of Bay Ridge Avenue on March 20, 1949. Note the 65th Street gas tanks in the background. (Tom Sarro Archives.)

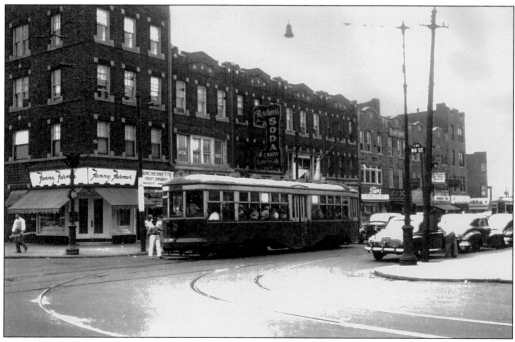

A trolley on 5th Avenue at 86th Street is seen here in 1948. (Tom Sarro Archives.)

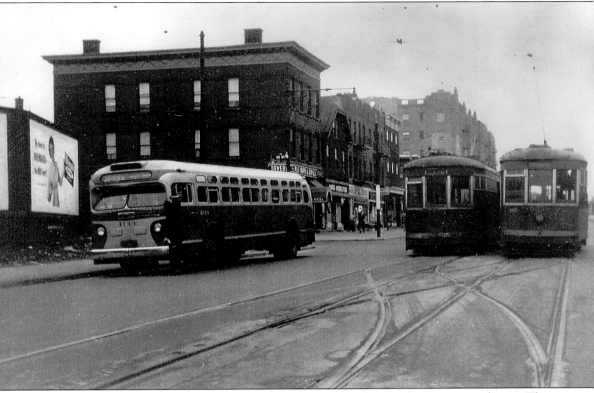

In 1949, 4th Avenue and 99th Street was a transit terminal. Yet, change was in the air. The 5th Avenue line trolleys 8293 and 8259 soon gave way to buses. Meanwhile, the driver of the 1948 GM bus prepares to start his run on the B37 3rd Avenue route, which was converted to buses in 1942. (Tom Sarro Archives.)

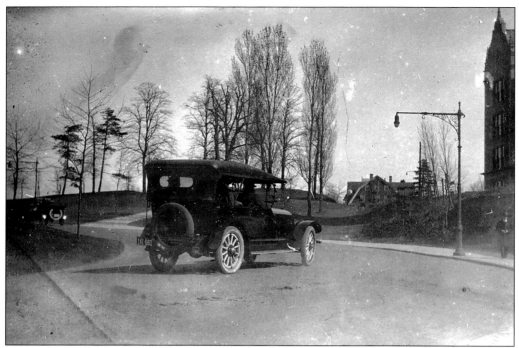

In this c. 1919 photograph, taken looking east on Shore Road Drive from 3rd Avenue near 67th Street, Bay Ridge High School is on the extreme right. (Courtesy of Doris Cruz.)

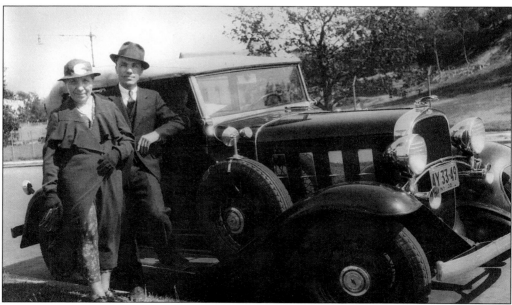

In the summer of 1935, longtime Bay Ridge resident George Peak and his mother pose on Shore Road near 68th Street with his first car: a 1931 Chevrolet two-door convertible. (Courtesy of Elaine LaTorre.)

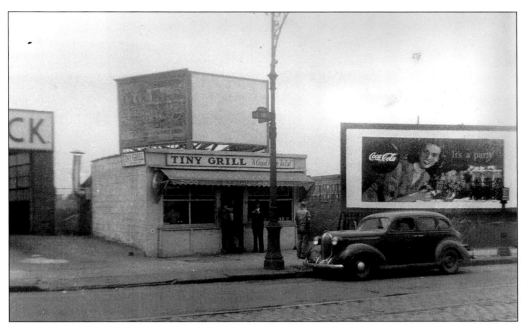

The Tiny Grill, "A Good Place to Eat" stood on 5th Avenue at 65th Street. Here, in 1946, the 5th Avenue trolleys rolled on the rails in the foreground and a customer has stepped out of his parked 1938 Plymouth—no traffic or parking problems then. This quiet corner was transformed when the elevated Gowanus Expressway opened above 65th Street in 1964. (George Manos.)

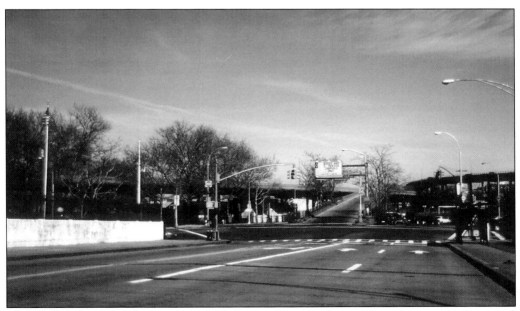

Looking north on 3rd Avenue from 65th Street, Samuel Winter Thomas recorded the arrival of the elevated railroad at this location in 1893. Later, the motor vehicle made its mark in Bay Ridge with the opening of the Belt Parkway viaduct (left) in 1941 and the Gowanus Expressway viaduct (right) in 1964. (Lawrence Stelter.)

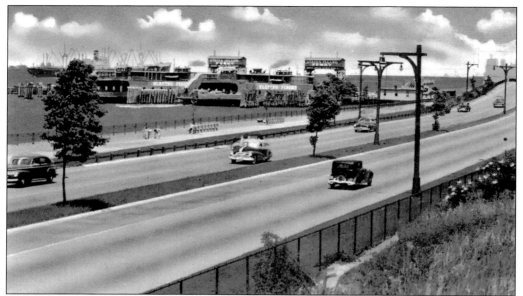

This is a 1940s view of the Belt Parkway and the 69th Street Ferry Terminal. (Peter Syrdahl.)

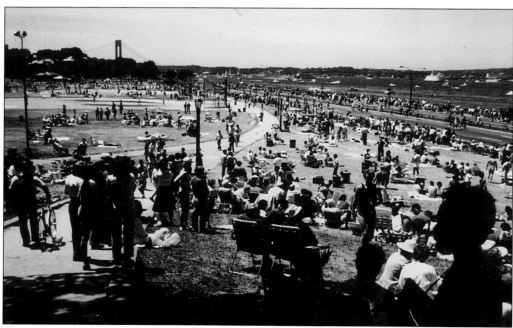

This view looks south into Shore Road Park from 72nd Street. Bay Ridge's spectacular view of the Narrows is a gift that is shared by all who live in or visit the community. Here, The bay is filled with nautical vessels and crowds of people are enjoying a beautiful, scenic day—a Bay Ridge scene reminiscent of what Samuel Winter Thomas also would have treasured and recorded more than a century ago. (Lawrence Stelter.)

Three

BAY RIDGE TO THE FUTURE: BUILDING THE VERRAZANO

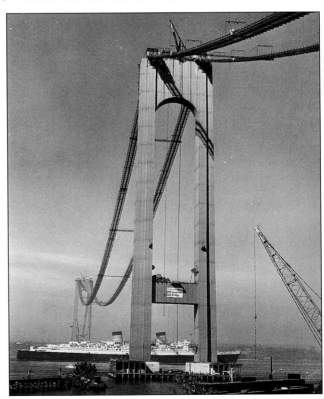

The S.S. *Queen Elizabeth* sails majestically into the New York harbor under the soon-to-be-completed Verrazano Bridge. (Peter Syrdahl.)

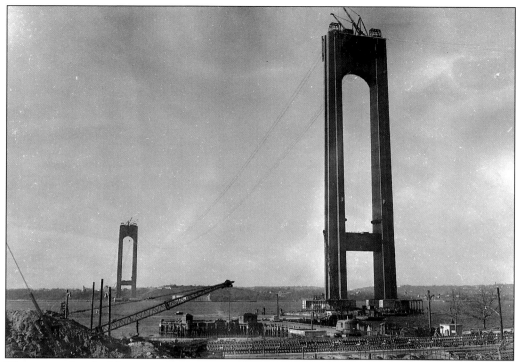

The towers for the Verrazano Bridge were completed in early 1963, and cable spinning began. (Photograph by Walter Wojtacki, courtesy of Eleanor Schiano.)

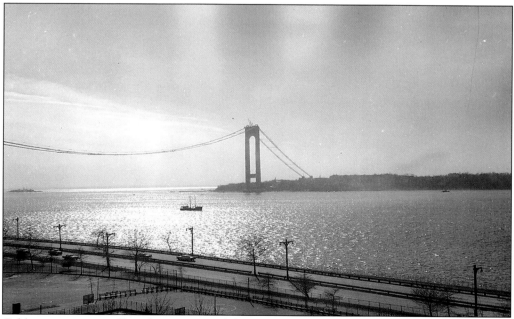

Cable spinning is well under way, as a fishing boat sails north through the Narrows in this mid-1963 photograph, taken looking south from Shore Road and 95th Street. (Photograph by Walter Wojtacki, courtesy of Eleanor Schiano.)

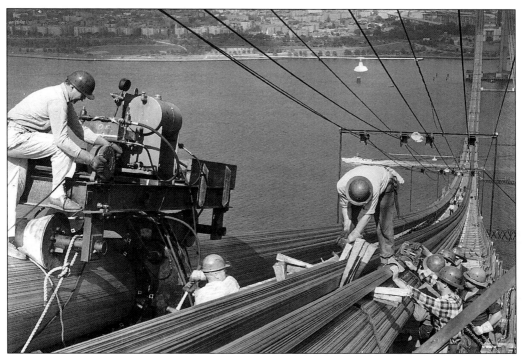

Construction workers are busy high atop the cables of the Verrazano Bridge. (Peter Syrdahl.)

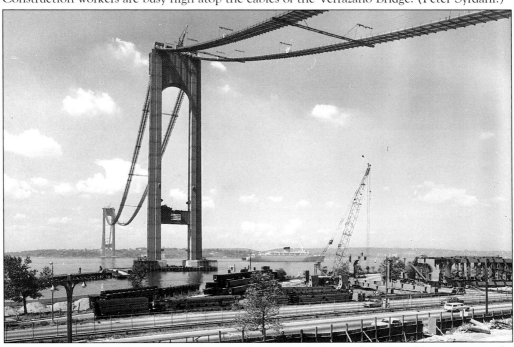

The Denyse pier and the remains of Fort Lafayette at the base of the Brooklyn tower can be seen in this photograph of the Verrazano Bridge. On the ground to the right is one of the large pieces of roadway decking, which was later lifted into place above. (Peter Syrdahl.)

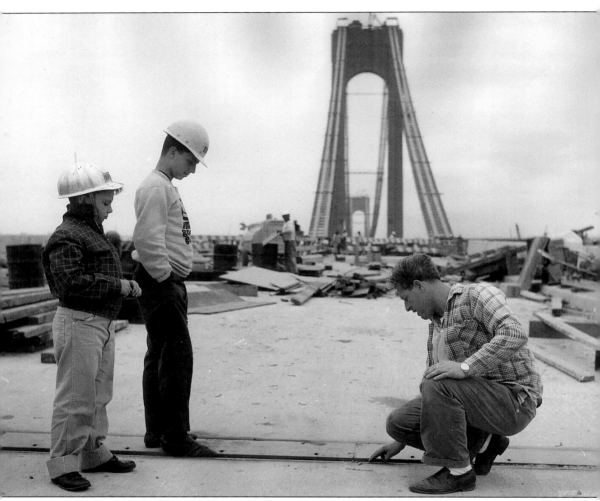

In 1963, 10-year-old Robert Wojtacki and his 14-year-old cousin Joseph Colabro go on a tour of the Brooklyn anchorage of the Verrazano Bridge. (Photograph by Walter Wojtacki, courtesy of Eleanor Schiano.)

Workmen near the top of the Verrazano Bridge celebrate their work with respect to the American flag. (Peter Syrdahl.)

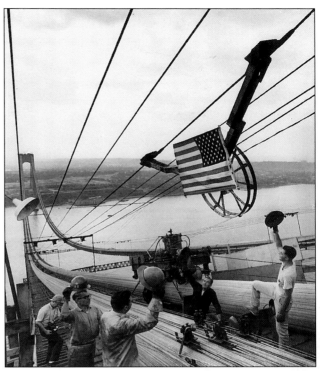

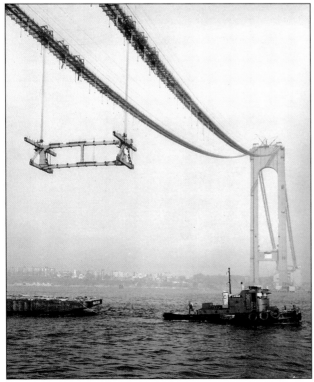

On October 25, 1963, the first piece of roadway deck is hoisted into place on the Verrazano Bridge. (Peter Syrdahl.)

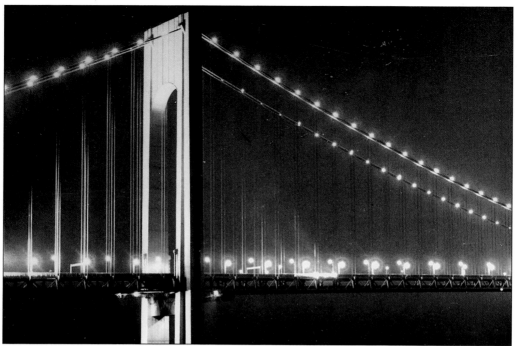

The Brooklyn tower of the Verrazano Bridge glows in the night c. 1965. (George Paszkewicz.)

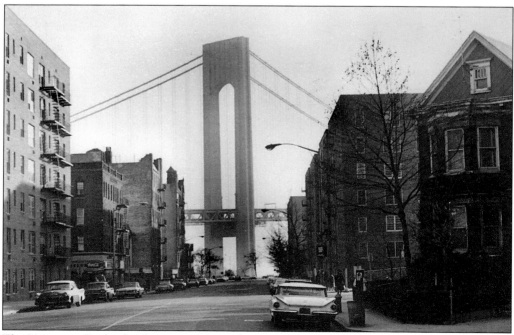

The Verrazano Bridge has become very much a part of the community's identity. It can be seen by looking south from virtually everywhere in Bay Ridge. This c. 1965 view along 3rd Avenue is from Marine Avenue. (George Paszkewicz.)